The *Book of Mormon*

LIVES OF GREAT RELIGIOUS BOOKS

The *Book of Mormon*

Paul C. Gutjahr

PRINCETON UNIVERSITY PRESS
Princeton and Oxford

Copyright © 2012 by Princeton University Press
Published by Princeton University Press, 41 William Street,
Princeton, New Jersey 08540
In the United Kingdom: Princeton University Press, 6 Oxford Street,
Woodstock, Oxfordshire OX20 1TW

press.princeton.edu

Jacket photograph: *Angel Moroni Salt Lake Temple.* © 2008 Thomas
Simpson | Focal-Point Photography

Library of Congress Cataloging-in-Publication Data

Gutjahr, Paul C., author.
    The Book of Mormon : a biography / Paul C. Gutjahr.
          pages cm — (Lives of great religious books)
    Includes bibliographical references and index.
    ISBN 978-0-691-14480-1 (hardcover : alk. paper)   1. Book
of Mormon—History.   2. Book of Mormon—Criticism,
interpretation, etc.   I. Title.   II. Series: Lives of great religious
books.
    BX8627.G88 2012
    289.3′22—dc23

                                        2011044063

British Library Cataloging-in-Publication Data is available

This book has been composed in Garamond Premier Pro

Printed on acid-free paper. ∞

Printed in the United States of America

10 9 8 7 6 5 4 3 2 1

For

Robert Eric Brown

(a.k.a. Bob)

A great scholar, but an even greater friend

Luke 8:15

This book must be either true or false. If true, it is one of the most important messages ever sent from God to man. If false, it is one of the most cunning, wicked, bold, deep-laid impositions ever palmed upon the world, calculated to deceive and ruin millions who will receive it as the word of God.

—ORSON PRATT, speaking of the *Book of Mormon*

CONTENTS

ILLUSTRATIONS

ACKNOWLEDGMENTS

My journey to writing this book has been a long one. The *Book of Mormon* first captured my attention in the eighth grade when an immensely kind and intelligent literature teacher by the name of Giles Florence Jr. introduced me to it. Neither of us could have predicted that that introduction would initiate my nearly forty-year quest to understand what was once described to the early Mormon apostle Parley Pratt as "a strange book, a VERY STRANGE BOOK!"

While Giles Florence may have been the first Mormon who befriended me, he certainly has not been the last. Countless others have followed in his footsteps, and many of those have done me great service in helping me write this book. Grant Smith, who suffered through graduate school with me, has been instrumental in bringing this book to completion. He carefully read and edited the entire manuscript before I submitted it to the Press. Not only is the book better because of his wisdom, but I am a better writer because of his unstinting generosity. Paul Westover also carefully read the manuscript, caught dozens of errors, made countless suggestions on how to improve the manuscript, and taught me a great deal I did not know about contemporary Mormon beliefs and practices. Also of help almost too great to measure was Grant Hardy, a scholar of such insight and generosity that I stand in awe of how much time and effort he put into this manuscript. Grant may not agree with all that fills the pages that follow, but I am convinced that it is a better book, and I am a better scholar, because of the time he invested in my work. These are debts I doubt I will ever be able to repay. These three scholars are living testimonies to the precious gift of academic fellowship and friendship.

In the course of my research, I was aided by countless members of the LDS Church in Utah. Rob Jex was a model of kindness and professionalism. Without his help, important sections of this book could not have been written. Others also offered invaluable aid: Gerald Argetsinger, Berne Broadbent, Tod Harris, Mark Jarman, Michael Landon, and Michael vonRosen. Jack Welch and David Whittaker at Brigham Young University proved invaluable in helping me find source and illustrative material. Even with all this help, I wish to in no way imply that the views in this book, or any mistakes therein, might be attributed to anyone but myself.

Friends outside the Church of Jesus Christ of Latter-day Saints helped as well. I had a terrific editor in Fred Appel, who offered me the chance to write this book and then patiently supported me throughout the entire process. He enlisted two wonderful reviewers to read my manuscript. Their comments made the book much better. Jonathan Elmer, Christoph Irmscher, Richard Nash, Steve Stein, and Nick Williams all lent a hand at various times to help improve this book. Madeleine Gonin, Cordah Pearce, and Alex Teschmacher patiently helped me get the illustrations in order. Alex Van Riesen, as always, was there as a friend offering humor and encouragement along the way. In countless ways, my life is richer because of Alex's presence in it.

This book also benefited from the financial generosity of several funding sources. The Charles Redd Center for Western Studies awarded me their Fellowship in Western American History, which allowed me to make two research trips to the L. Tom Perry Special Collections of the Harold B. Lee Library at Brigham Young University. Indiana University also supported this project with two separate grants: a Research Grant-in-Aid from the College of Arts and Sciences to help with the costs of illustrations, and a Summer Research Fellowship from the Office of the Vice Provost for Research, which enabled me to dedicate a summer to writing this book.

While other individuals and institutions have shown great kindness in helping bring this book to completion, my family continues to be my greatest source of support. My wife, Cathy, and my two sons have all had to make sacrifices to help me complete my research on this book, and my gratitude and love for them exceed my every ability to put into words. My parents, and my sister, Karen, have also always been stalwart pillars of support. They continue to be my life's greatest models of generosity and unconditional love.

Finally, I dedicate this book to Bob Brown. Bob has been a close friend since our graduate school days together at the University of Iowa. For over two decades, he has been a listening ear, an insightful critic, and a faithful friend. We have suffered together through bad graduate seminars, terrible movies, not-so-festive strawberry festivals, and various office-remodeling projects completed under the cover of darkness. We have also shared dreams, moves, home improvement projects, vacations, as well as rounds of golf on some of the most run-down courses in the Midwest. True friends in life are rare. Rarer still are friends as kind, intelligent, and encouraging as Bob. Even as I type these words, I cannot help but smile. That is what Bob brings out in people: peace and joy. May this slender volume stand as a token of gratitude for a treasured friend who has enriched my life, the lives of my family, and my scholarly work in ways too numerous to count.

Bloomington, Indiana
August 2011

Members of the Church of Jesus Christ of Latter-day Saints have a long tradition of referring to Joseph Smith Jr. simply as "Joseph." Since my book involves a great many Smiths—including Alvin, Hyrum, William, Samuel, Lucy, Emma, Ethan, Joseph Smith Sr., and Joseph Smith III—I have chosen to refer to Mormonism's founding prophet as "Joseph" for the sake of clarity.

Germination

PART I

Now, we will compare the word unto a seed

[which] may be planted in your heart

—Alma 32:28

Prologue

In 1828, the directors of the twelve-year-old American Bible Society (ABS) set forth the audacious plan to provide every American household with a Bible. In a nation where only twenty years earlier publishers had been hard-pressed to produce two thousand copies of any given book, the ABS exerted its formidable will to undertake a breathtaking mission it named "The General Supply."[1] Between 1829 and 1831 the ABS published and distributed an astounding half million copies of the scriptures in an attempt to touch the lives of each and every American with the word of God. In this way, the Bible became part of the very foundation of antebellum American print culture.

While the ABS was seeking to bury the country under a mound of Bibles, a young farmer and day laborer named Joseph Smith Jr. was busy with a mound of his own. Claiming angelic guidance,

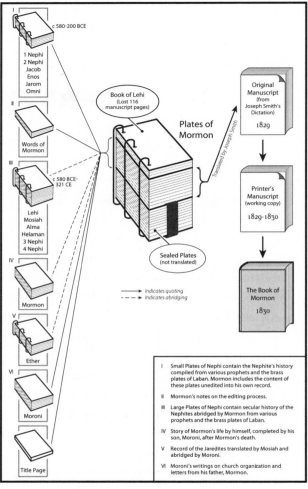

I c 580-200 BCE

1 Nephi
2 Nephi
Jacob
Enos
Jarom
Omni

Book of Lehi
(Lost 116
manuscript pages)

Plates of
Mormon

II

Words of
Mormon

III c 580 BCE-
321 CE

Lehi
Mosiah
Alma
Helaman
3 Nephi
4 Nephi

Sealed Plates
(not translated)

IV

Mormon

V

Ether

VI

Moroni

Title Page

Translated by Joseph Smith

Original
Manuscript
(from
Joseph Smith's
Dictation)
1829

Printer's
Manuscript
(working copy)
1829-1830

The Book of
Mormon
1830

⟶ Indicates quoting
– – ⟶ Indicates abridging

I   Small Plates of Nephi contain the Nephite's history
    compiled from various prophets and the brass
    plates of Laban. Mormon includes the content of
    these plates unedited into his own record.

II Mormon's notes on the editing process.

III Large Plates of Nephi contain secular history of the
    Nephites abridged by Mormon from various
    prophets and the brass plates of Laban.

IV Story of Mormon's life by himself, completed by his
    son, Moroni, after Mormon's death.

V   Record of the Jaredites translated by Mosiah and
    abridged by Moroni.

VI Moroni's writings on church organization and
    letters from his father, Mormon.

Chart of the different sets of plates adapted from "Book of
Mormon Plates and Records," in *Reexploring the Book of
Mormon*, ed. John W. Welch (Provo, UT: FARMS, 1992), 17.

Joseph unearthed a set of golden plates from a hill near his upstate New York home. Joseph would later announce that these were the *Plates of Mormon*, named after a fourth-century prophet and scribe. Mormon had set down the history of several once-mighty ancient American civilizations by copying, abridging, and adding to the records of scribes who for centuries had recorded the history of these peoples. Especially important for Mormon's editorial and authorial purposes were the *Plates of Nephi* (which actually comprised two sets of plates known as the "Small Plates of Nephi" and the "Large Plates of Nephi") and the *Plates of Ether.* Through considerable effort and hardship, Joseph translated the "Reformed Egyptian" writing he found on the *Plates of Mormon*, transforming their message into a new sacred scripture: the *Book of Mormon*.

When the *Book of Mormon* first appeared in 1830, it echoed the Bible in many ways. It was a small, yet imposing, octavo volume containing nearly six hundred pages of text.[2] Its size and binding style strikingly resembled the most common Bible editions then being passionately produced and distributed by the ABS, and its narrative was full of religious ritual, sacred commandments, and wondrous stories of divine intervention.[3]

The *Book of Mormon* differed from the Bible in other ways, offering information found nowhere in

THE

BOOK OF MORMON:

AN ACCOUNT WRITTEN BY THE HAND OF MOR-
MON, UPON PLATES TAKEN FROM
THE PLATES OF NEPHI.

Wherefore it is an abridgment of the Record of the People of Nephi; and also of the Lamanites: written to the Lamanites, which are a remnant of the House of Israel; and also to Jew and Gentile: written by way of commandment, and also by the spirit of Prophesy and of Revelation. Written, and sealed up, and hid up unto the LORD, that they might not be destroyed; to come forth by the gift and power of GOD, unto the interpretation thereof; sealed by the hand of Moroni, and hid up unto the LORD, to come forth in due time by the way of Gentile; the interpretation thereof by the gift of GOD; an abridgment taken from the Book of Ether.

Also, which is a Record of the People of Jared, which were scattered at the time the LORD confounded the language of the people when they were building a tower to get to Heaven: which is to shew unto the remnant of the House of Israel how great things the LORD hath done for their fathers; and that they may know the covenants of the LORD, that they are not cast off forever; and also to the convincing of the Jew and Gentile that JESUS is the CHRIST, the ETERNAL GOD, manifesting Himself unto all nations. And now if there be fault, it be the mistake of men; wherefore condemn not the things of GOD, that ye may be found spotless at the judgment seat of CHRIST.

BY JOSEPH SMITH, JUNIOR,
AUTHOR AND PROPRIETOR.

PALMYRA:
PRINTED BY E. B. GRANDIN, FOR THE AUTHOR.

1830.

Title page from the first edition of the *Book of Mormon* (1830), including Joseph Smith Jr.'s identification of himself as the work's "author and proprietor." Courtesy Lilly Library, Indiana University, Bloomington, IN the traditional biblical narrative. It tells the story of three family groups who travel from the ancient Middle East to the Americas. A small portion of the book traces the history of Jared and his descendants from their departure after the failure of the Tower of Babel around 2500 BCE to their decline around 300 BCE.[4] The majority of the book's content describes the family of Lehi, who left "the land of Jerusalem" around 600 BCE.[5] This family divides into warring factions named after two of Lehi's sons: Nephi and Laman. Around 420 CE, the Lamanites destroy the Nephites only to see their own civilization collapse. The few Lamanite survivors will later evolve into various Native American tribes. The last group, led by Mulek, is barely mentioned. It travels to the Americas at roughly the same time as Lehi and eventually merges with the Nephites.

In all, the plates that Joseph used for his translation claimed to offer a historical account that began around the middle of the third millennium BCE and reached up to roughly the fifth century CE. They are named after one of the Nephites' final scribes, Mormon, who is represented as having done the greater part of the work of writing, editing, and redacting a large collection of records into the set of plates that Joseph later translated. Mormon's work was completed by his son Moroni, the last known survivor of the once-great Nephite nation. After finishing his work, Moroni buried the plates in what later came to be known as the Hill Cumorah, a prominent point of elevated land near Joseph's upstate New York home. In the early 1820s, centuries after his death, Moroni appeared to Joseph in angelic form, announcing that God had chosen Joseph to recover and translate the *Plates of Mormon* so that a new age of revelation might begin on the earth.

One of the most distinctive elements of the *Book of Mormon* is its Old Testament historical feel coupled with a distinct focus on Jesus Christ, thereby conflating the Christian Bible's Old and New Testaments. On its title page, the *Book of Mormon* announces that it exists, in part, to convince "the Jew and Gentile that JESUS is the CHRIST, the ETERNAL GOD, manifesting Himself unto all nations."[6] Undergirding this self-proclaimed mandate, the volume records revelations given to the Nephites as early as 600 BCE concerning the birth, life, and sacrificial death of Jesus as the Messiah.[7] The *Book of Mormon*'s Christology is complex and detailed. It reaches its fullest manifestation in Jesus appearing to the Nephites after his death and resurrection in the Middle East. Descending from heaven, a man clad in white announces, "I am Jesus Christ, whom the prophets testified shall come into the world."[8] The Nephites then bear witness to the spear wound in his side and the nail marks in his hands and feet before Jesus goes on to minister to them by delivering a discourse similar to the Sermon on the Mount, healing their sick, blessing their children, instituting the rite of the Lord's Supper, and bestowing special authority and power on a chosen twelve. Thus the Christ of the Eastern Hemisphere also becomes the Christ of the Western Hemisphere, a savior to the entire world.[9]

No matter whether one considers the *Book of Mormon* to be divinely inspired holy writ or the work of one man's impressive imagination, it is increasingly hard to argue against the growing scholarly consensus that "the Book of Mormon should rank among the great achievements of American literature."[10] While the book stands as an important artifact in the study of the American history and culture, it is no less important as a contemporary religious text with global influence.[11] The book can now be read by nearly 90 percent of the world's inhabitants in their native languages.[12] Enjoying ever larger print runs in its nearly two-century history, the *Book of Mormon* achieved a distribution of 150 million copies worldwide by 2011.[13] Changes in American publishing in the late twentieth century have allowed for exponential growth in producing the *Book of Mormon.* Computer technology has helped translate the book into dozens of languages and has expedited the printing of more than 50 million copies of the book in the last ten years alone.

Such massive publishing statistics lend credence to the religious historian Rodney Stark's argument that, given the right conditions, by the mid-twenty-first century Mormonism might "achieve a worldwide following comparable to that of Islam, Buddhism, Christianity, Hinduism, and the other dominant world faiths."[14] Whether or not Stark's projection proves correct, it is obvious that the book that gave the Church of Jesus Christ of Latter-day Saints its popular name might be considered the most important religious text ever to emerge from the United States.

What lies before you is a biography of the *Book of Mormon*, a study that examines the sacred book's journey from a small print shop in antebellum Palmyra, New York, through its dozens of editions in English and more than one hundred translations. This book also examines the transformations of the *Book of Mormon* into other media such as children's books, comic books, motion pictures, and elaborately staged pageants.[15] Richard Bushman, in his remarkable biography of Joseph Smith Jr., observed that the first edition of the *Book of Mormon* was an "unusually spare production," but once released the book quickly took on "a life of its own."[16] What follows is the story of that life.

Joseph's Gold Bible

The story of the *Book of Mormon* cannot be separated from its self-proclaimed "author and proprietor," Joseph Smith Jr.[1] The fifth child born into the farming family of Joseph and Lucy Mack Smith, Joseph Jr. entered the world two days before Christmas, 1805, in the small town of Sharon, Vermont. In an era when children provided critical labor for a farm's viability, the Smith family eventually grew to include six sons and three daughters. By the time Joseph was ten, his family had already moved several times, a tortuous migratory pattern that began after Joseph's father sold his long-established Vermont farm to settle a debt he had incurred speculating on a cargo of ginseng sent to China. In the coming years, the Smith family migrated from one farm to another, drifting ever farther west to cheaper and less developed tracts of land. Eventually relocating to the burgeoning town of Palmyra, New York, Joseph's father once

This image of Joseph Smith Jr. is the standard portrait of the prophet encountered by all who read the most recent missionary editions of the *Book of Mormon*. Courtesy of the Church Archives, The Church of Jesus Christ of Latter-day Saints

again attempted to start anew by working his own land and letting his sons out as day laborers.

In the opening years of the nineteenth century, Palmyra and its surrounding countryside stood on the farthest edge of the nation's rapidly expanding frontier. From 1790 to 1820, upstate New York grew from roughly 350,000 to nearly 1.4 million inhabitants, and yet for all the promises the region held out to those wishing to make a new life for themselves, uncleared land, harsh weather, and poor roads made farm failure and debilitating poverty ever-present threats.[2] Complete economic collapse hovered so constantly at the Smith doorstep that Joseph's father became interested (and got Joseph interested as well) in seeking hidden treasure using divining rods and other magical instruments in vain attempts to gain riches from the earth in ways other than farming. In Palmyra, just as they had done on numerous farms before, the Smiths led difficult and dispiriting lives.

While Joseph Smith Sr. turned to treasure hunting to alleviate his family's precarious economic situation, Lucy Mack Smith found her solace in religion. She joined the local Presbyterian congregation and encouraged her family to seek comfort and guidance in faith.[3] It was a time of particularly fervent religious activity on the New York frontier as the region was filled with all manner of revivalist preachers, missionaries, and other spiritual entrepreneurs. Baptists, Methodists, Quakers, Shakers, Congregationalists, Presbyterians, Episcopalians, and Universalists all competed for the attention and religious loyalty of people desperate to make a living off land that only a few years before had been largely untouched by the plow.[4] Palmyra was not immune to the region's pulsating religious fervor. In 1808 during a Baptist revival, one hundred Palmyrans converted, a number so large that it necessitated the building of a meeting hall for the hamlet's new believers.[5]

Central to the spiritual vision of many of those wishing to spread the Gospel on New York's hardscrabble frontier was the promise that every individual could experience an unmediated and personal relationship with an omnipotent God. Such a relationship was often confirmed through dreams, fits, visions, and trances. While power might be wrested daily from their hands through the acts of relentless rent collectors, heartless shopkeepers, and disreputable land agents, many frontiersmen and women found themselves able to commune with a God who not only cared about their problems but also wielded the power to offer meaningful aid. Those who participated in camp meetings and other religious services took great comfort in the fact that God frequently revealed his presence and power through physical healing, electric-like pulses of ecstatic joy, or prophetic visions of the future. Just as those in the early Christian Church had been able to hold regular and direct discourse with God, many on the New York frontier experienced a similar, life-changing access to the Almighty.[6]

In this spiritually vibrant culture, the young Joseph experienced his own highly personal encounter with God at the age of fourteen. Long interested in religion, Joseph had begun to read his Bible regularly at the age of twelve and even joined the probationary class at the local Methodist church, hoping for his own heartfelt experience of religion. He ended up confused and disenchanted with the religious enthusiasm that surrounded him.[7] In an effort to bring clarity to his spiritual quest, he decided to take the Bible at its word when it encouraged, "If any of you lack wisdom, let him ask of God" (James 1:5). Joseph retreated to the woods near his home to ask God which one of the many competing religious sects actually taught his truths.[8] In an event later christened "The First Vision," Joseph claimed that God the Father and his son, Jesus Christ, had appeared and forbade him to join any of the religious bodies in the region.[9] They instructed him to wait for an angelic visitation that would lead him to true faith.

According to Joseph, these promises were fulfilled three years later on September 21, 1823, when a floating, white-robed angelic figure named Moroni visited him in his room late one night.[10] Moroni told him that there was a "book deposited, written upon gold plates," that gave an account of the former inhabitants of the American continent and also taught "the fulness of the everlasting Gospel" as Jesus had delivered it to those ancient people.[11] Although Joseph was allowed to glimpse the plates the day after Moroni's initial appearance, he was not permitted to remove them immediately from their centuries-old hiding place. Only four years later did Moroni allow Joseph to remove the plates, which had been buried under a stone slab on a hill roughly three miles south of his family's Palmyra farm. Later the hill would come to be known as "Cumorah" after a location named in the *Book of Mormon*. In the months that followed, Joseph learned that he was to translate only a portion of the plates. Certain plates containing prophecies of the future were to remain sealed until a time "when the people of the Lord are prepared, and found worthy."[12]

Joseph had taken along with him his new bride, Emma, when he set out to recover the plates just after the stroke of midnight on September 22, 1827. He found the stone slab, levered it off with a sturdy stick, and recovered the plates along with an ancient breastplate and two stones called "interpreters." The interpreters were set in eyeglass-like frames that could be attached to the breastplate.[13] The whole apparatus was later referred to as the Old Testament divination tool called the "Urim and Thummim."[14] Joseph and Emma returned to the Smith farm, but not before hiding the plates in an old hollowed-out birch log along the way.

The safety of the plates was a primary concern for Joseph from the moment he unearthed them.[15] The birch log was but the first of a series of hiding places he found for the plates as he settled on the best way to begin translating them. In the days that followed, Joseph's mother, Lucy, helped him commission a local cabinetmaker to build a cherry-wood chest to hold them.[16] Joseph transferred the plates to the chest and then constantly moved the chest around the farm to keep it out of the hands of robbers. What came to be known throughout the area as Joseph's "Gold Bible" proved to be a sore temptation for an ever-growing number of treasure hunters intent on making their fortune by stealing Joseph's golden plates.[17] For the next three years Joseph waged a constant battle to protect the plates from others who had more interest in their gold than in their spiritual substance.

Joseph quickly realized that he would need financial help if he were ever going to find the time to translate and raise the capital to publish the plates' message. He turned to one of Palmyra's wealthier citizens, a farmer named Martin Harris, for help. Harris had frequently given Joseph work on his farm just a mile north of Palmyra, and he was known by his neighbors as a kind, if somewhat religiously enthusiastic, man.[18] Upon first broaching the topic of the plates, Joseph informed Harris that an angel had appointed the farmer to be a special aide to his translation work. Harris went home, retired to his bedroom, and prayed about Joseph's proposition. His prayers were quickly answered, for in a "still small voice spoken in the soul" Harris felt that the Lord told him that the plates were indeed "designed to bring in the fullness of [God's] gospel."[19] He accepted Joseph's commission.

Because others in Palmyra were so insistent on seeing the plates—to the point that a mob declared its intention to tar and feather Joseph if he would not show them his newfound treasure—Joseph decided to take the plates and translation stones to Emma's parents' farm in Harmony, Pennsylvania, some 135 miles southeast of Palmyra. Stealing away late one evening with the plates hidden in a barrel of beans, Joseph and Emma surreptitiously journeyed to Harmony. Complicating an already long and difficult journey was the fact that Emma was now pregnant with the couple's first child. When they arrived, they found Emma's father, Isaac Hale, highly skeptical of the existence, much less the message, of Joseph's plates. Joseph allowed Hale to heft the box that contained the plates, but did not allow him to see the plates themselves.[20] Hale was incensed by this secrecy and demanded that Joseph find honest work if he wished to stay in his home. Over the next few months Joseph simultaneously worked his father-in-law's land and attempted to carve out time to translate the plates.

Translating the plates was no easy task, and as Joseph began the work, he struggled to find a method to reveal the plates' message. In the earliest days of the translation endeavor, Joseph worked with Emma to draw as precisely as possible a few of the characters he found on the plates. Just two months after his move to Harmony, Martin Harris arrived in Harmony announcing that God had told him of the significance of Joseph's translation work, and proffering his help. At intermittent intervals over the next year and a half, the two men worked together to transcribe the plates. At one point, Harris even took samples of the figures Joseph had copied from the plates, along with their accompanying translations, and sought out leading ancient-language scholars in Utica, Albany, and New York City who might be able to confirm, and possibly even aid them in, their work.[21]

Reports differ concerning to whom exactly Harris showed these facsimiles and what their conclusions were. The most famous individual he consulted was Charles Anthon, professor of classical studies at Columbia College in New York City. Anthon later claimed that he had verified neither Joseph's transcriptions nor his preliminary translation work. Harris, on the other hand, claimed that Anthon had fully confirmed Joseph's work, but then withdrew his endorsement once he learned that the figures came from golden plates unearthed by a poor farmer in upstate New York. Anthon demanded to see the original plates, something that Harris told him was impossible. Anthon then famously declared that he could not read a "sealed book," a statement that Joseph later claimed to be a fulfillment of the Isaiah passage that told of a "book that is sealed, which men deliver to one that is learned, saying, Read this I pray thee, and he saith, I cannot; for it is sealed" (Isa. 29:11).[22] Undeterred by Anthon's skepticism, Harris returned to Joseph utterly convinced of the authenticity of the message the golden plates contained.[23]

Upon Harris's return, the two men sat down anew to translate the plates, moving from concentrating on copying the plates' intricate symbols to depending ever more heavily on the "interpreters," and later a single seer stone (which he had found while digging a well for one of his Palmyra neighbors in 1822), to guide the translation. From April through June of 1828, the two men sat at a table with a curtain dividing them as Joseph used the "interpreters" to painstakingly dictate the plates' message. By the middle of June, they had translated 116 pages of what later became known as the Book of Lehi. The work was so arduous, and Joseph's claims at times so unbelievable, that Harris began to question once again whether Joseph was indeed translating ancient plates or simply making a fool of him in order to swindle him out of his money. As the work proceeded, Harris repeatedly asked to see the plates, and repeatedly Joseph refused. Not even granted a glimpse of the plates, Harris began to doubt the entire endeavor.

Nursing his own doubts and stinging from the persistent skepticism of his wife, Harris began to beg that he might at least be permitted to take the manuscript home to show his family. Harris's wife had long believed the worst of Joseph. She did not credit the plates' existence, and repeatedly told her husband that all Joseph wanted was to cheat him out of his wealth.[24] At last Joseph relented and told Harris that he had received divine permission for Harris to show the manuscript to five members of his closest family: his wife, his brother, his parents, and his sister-in-law. Joseph, however, remained uneasy about releasing the manuscript and required that Harris take a solemn oath that he would carefully guard the work and reveal it only to the five people he had named. Harris readily agreed and eagerly set off for his home with the manuscript.

The decision proved a disastrous one. Upon arriving at his home in Palmyra, Harris locked the manuscript in a bureau drawer. The pages seemingly placated his wife, and, encouraged by having tangible evidence to support his claims concerning Joseph and the importance of their work together, Harris began to show the manuscript to people not named in the covenant he had made with Joseph. Soon, he was showing the manuscript to any visitor who happened to stop at his home. In a matter of days, the manuscript disappeared. No one is sure what became of it, but Joseph's mother, Lucy, suspected Harris's wife of stealing the manuscript to destroy it or alter it in such a way that if Joseph chose to retranslate the section, she would be able to expose the work as a fraud by pointing to discrepancies between the original translation and a later one.[25]

To make matters worse, Joseph had been required to return the plates and the "interpreters" to Moroni soon after he handed over the manuscript to Harris. With the loss of the manuscript, and now bereft of the plates and the means to translate them, Joseph feared that he had forfeited his divine appointment as revelator of a new Gospel. It was only when Joseph received a revelation chastising him for his carelessness, but assuring him that he would continue to serve as God's revelatory instrument, that he found some measure of peace.[26] The plates and the "interpreters" were returned to him on September 22, 1828, the date of Moroni's annual visitation, and the way was once again open to Joseph to become the means of bringing forth a new sacred scripture.

During the following winter, Joseph's work on the translation slowed to a crawl as he spent the majority of his time tending to a small farm he had recently purchased. Emma replaced Harris as her husband's principal scribe, sometimes aided by Joseph's younger brother Samuel. Working with Emma, Joseph did not begin his translation at the same point he had earlier. Instead, he took up the translation with Emma where he and Harris had stopped (somewhere around the first part of the Book of Mosiah). As they worked, Joseph removed the curtain between him and Emma. The plates simply sat on the table between them, although they remained hidden from view, wrapped in a linen tablecloth. Emma never saw the plates, but she did feel them, later reporting that they gave off a metallic sound when she thumbed them like pages in a book.[27] Throughout the translation process, she sat in awe of Joseph's ability to dictate such a complex work. She sat patiently for hours receiving his dictation and later recalled that when they took breaks to eat or do chores, he invariably resumed the story exactly where he had left off without referring to the manuscript they had just transcribed or any other material.[28]

Emma also claimed that no other book was near them as he dictated God's message. She steadfastly maintained that he could not have hidden such a book from her. Joseph simply used the "interpreters" or a seer stone placed in a hat as he dictated twenty to thirty words at a time. In explaining the later stages of the translation process, Joseph told of words that glowed to life in the seer stone itself. Joseph Knight, a local farmer who witnessed this portion of the translation process, recounted that Joseph saw the words "apper in Brite Roman Letters. Then he would tell the writer and he would write it. Then that would go away the next sentance would Come and so on."[29] Examining the stone buried in his hat, Joseph recited each of the revealed words, and he also spelled out the more difficult names of people and places.[30] Later, Joseph dictated at times without the plates' even being present.

The pace of the translation work increased radically in April 1829 when Oliver Cowdery, an occasional schoolteacher and ardent religious enthusiast, appeared on Joseph's doorstep, having heard of the plates and wanting to know more. Cowdery had traveled from Vermont, where his family's pastor, Ethan Smith, had become a local celebrity by publishing a book entitled *View of the Hebrews* (1823).[31] In it, Smith argued that Native Americans were descended from the lost tribes of Israel. Cowdery was almost certainly familiar with the book, and it probably catalyzed his passionate interest in Joseph's manuscript, which also posited a link between Native Americans and the ancient Hebrews. Joseph soon convinced Cowdery of the importance of the plates and had him replace Emma as his primary scribe.

Together the two men embarked on an astoundingly prolific period of translation work. Over the space of just three months (April through June),

Cowdery—with occasional help from others—copied down 3,500 words a day as Joseph dictated the remaining contents of the plates.[32] In June of 1829, Joseph, seeking a place where he could finish the translation without distractions, moved with Emma and Cowdery to Fayette, New York (roughly twenty-seven miles southeast of Palmyra), to take up residence at Peter Whitmer Sr.'s farm. Joseph was an acquaintance of Whitmer, but Peter's son, David, was a good friend of Cowdery's. Unlike their homestead near Emma's parents, the Whitmer farm offered Joseph the solitude and focus he needed to complete the translation. The Whitmer family quickly became enthusiastic supporters of Joseph's translation work.

As they neared the end of their work on the plates, Joseph once again had to confront Harris's loss of 116 manuscript pages. After praying for guidance concerning how best to handle these lost pages, Joseph reportedly received a revelation that he was not to retranslate this particular portion of the plates. Doubters might use contradictions between manuscripts to discredit the work as a whole if the missing 116 pages ever reappeared. Instead, Joseph was instructed to translate a new set of plates he later identified as the "Small Plates of Nephi" that contained the books of Nephi, Jacob, Enos, Jarom, and Omni and covered roughly the same events recorded in the now lost Book of Lehi.

During this frenetic, final period of translation, Joseph also had to deal with Cowdery's increasing desire to act not only as the project's scribe, but as a translator as well. Joseph answered Cowdery's pleas by telling him that he would indeed be given the ability to translate the plates if he would only be patient and earnestly wait upon the Lord for the gift.[33] Cowdery did, in fact, eventually try his hand at translation, but found himself unable to replicate Joseph's success with either the seer stone or the Urim and Thummim. Joseph remained the sole translator of the plates.

Joseph had so jealously guarded the plates that even his most sympathetic associates began to doubt their actual existence as the translation process unfolded. While some had touched the plates either by lifting boxes that held them or feeling their outline under a cloth cover, Joseph was the only person who could say that he had actually seen them. To reassure those around him and give his claims greater credibility, Joseph agreed to take three of his closest supporters—Oliver Cowdery, David Whitmer, and Martin Harris—into the woods to pray, to inquire whether they might be allowed to see the plates. As the four men knelt in prayer, nothing happened. After a fruitless period of waiting, Harris dismissed himself, declaring that he lacked the faith to be granted the gift of seeing the plates. After

The three witnesses to the golden plates as pictured atop the Hill Cumorah where the angel Moroni directed Joseph Smith Jr. to uncover the plates. From the *Contributor* 5 (1883): 35; courtesy of Neal A. Maxwell Institute for Religious Scholarship, Brigham Young University he left, an angel holding the plates appeared to the others. Cowdery later reported: "I beheld with my eyes. And handled with my hands the gold plates from which it was translated. I also beheld the Interpreters."[34] Joseph then went in search of Harris, whom he found deeper in the woods. He prayed with Harris, and the two men were then visited by the same angel and shown the same plates.

Just days later, Joseph widened the circle of witnesses by showing the plates to an additional eight men (all of whom later skeptics complained were members of either the Smith or the Whitmer family).[35] These eight men were allowed to see and handle the plates without the aid of an angel. Joseph attached the testimonies of these eleven men at the end of the first published version of the *Book of Mormon* to bear witness to "all nations, kindreds, tongues, and people, unto whom this work shall come" that he was not the only man who had "seen the plates which contain this record."[36] After he finished his translation work, Joseph claimed that the angel Moroni took back the plates, making him and these eleven witnesses the only people in the modern era ever to see this ancient golden record.

Now came the time to find a publisher for the work, and Joseph faced a double challenge. He needed to find someone willing to print an alleged new sacred scripture, and he needed the funds to pay for the work. A local printer in Palmyra, Egbert B. Grandin, initially balked at the opportunity to publish Joseph's mammoth manuscript.[37] He worried about the massive size of the project (six hundred pages in printed form), about getting paid, and about the response of his Protestant neighbors if he agreed to print a book that questioned traditional Protestant beliefs. This last concern is not to be underestimated. Grandin lived in a revival-soaked community where the Bible reigned as the preeminent, often unquestioned, divine text. Joseph's book promised to significantly challenge the beliefs of those who revered the Bible with its claim to be a revelation that was every bit as divinely inspired and authoritative as their treasured sacred text. Grandin needed to think long and hard before becoming the publisher of a text many would consider an upstart rival to, and thus critique of, the book American Christians held most dear.

Eventually, Grandin did agree to print the book. All the reasons for his change of heart may never be known, but his course reversal came, in part, because Martin Harris guaranteed payment for the book's printing costs and Grandin discovered that another printer, located in Rochester, New York, was willing to undertake the work. If nothing else, Grandin was a pragmatist. If the book's publication was inevitable, he was willing to risk the ire of his neighbors. Grandin was enough of a businessman to not let work and money go to another printer if he could obtain the commission himself.

Harris mortgaged his farm as a security for the three thousand dollars Grandin demanded to produce five thousand copies of the book. Lucy, Harris's wife, was absolutely livid. She was convinced that Joseph had finally accomplished what he had always intended to do, get her husband's money. She soon left her husband, and, as it turned out, her predictions of financial ruin were well-founded. Once the book was published, it sold so slowly that Harris was forced to sell his farm to settle the unpaid balance of publication costs.

Joseph submitted a title page for the *Book of Mormon* on June 11, 1829, to obtain a copyright for the work, and Grandin hired John Gilbert, another local printer, in August of that year to begin typesetting the book. Grandin, however, was not the first person to publish portions of the *Book of Mormon*. During the typesetting, a Palmyran named Abner Cole obtained some loose pages of the book and, under the pseudonym O. Dogberry, began to publish excerpts of it in his new weekly periodical, the *Reflector*.[38] Joseph personally intervened to stop Cole's work, warning him of the penalties for infringing upon his established copyright. After printing two issues that contained excerpts from the Book of Nephi, Cole desisted.[39]

As if pirated copies of the book were not trouble enough for Grandin, opposition to the work grew in Palmyra. Rumors circulated that men were eager to obtain the manuscript in order to destroy it, and Grandin worried about his personal safety and the safety of his print shop. More than a few townspeople tried to convince him to abandon the work, vowing never to buy a copy of the book. Threats against the book also worried Joseph, who, still haunted by the loss of the 116 pages he had entrusted to Harris's care, instructed Cowdery to recopy the entire manuscript to safeguard the translation. Ultimately, Cowdery's second copy came to be known as the "Printer's Manuscript," and Joseph instructed that the Original and Printer's Manuscripts never be in Grandin's print shop at the same time. Gilbert typeset most of the *Book of Mormon* from the Printer's Manuscript until roughly the last sixth of the book, when Cowdery fell behind in his copying work and Gilbert was forced to use the Original Manuscript.[40] As a final precaution, Joseph ordered that anyone carrying manuscript pages between the Smith farm and the printing office not travel alone.

It is notable that although the manuscript was closely and legibly written, it contained precious few punctuation marks from beginning to end. Gilbert became almost totally responsible for punctuating the text as he typeset it. Joseph came to the print shop to revel in the appearance of the first pages of the book, but after his initial interest in the printing process, he largely left the details and editing of the manuscript to Cowdery and Gilbert.[41] Cowdery even learned to set type in order to help see the book published.

In March 1830, the book was finally finished, and Grandin began to advertise it for sale. The area's boycott proved unusually effective, and hundreds of copies languished in Grandin's storeroom. Martin Harris, who had struck a deal with the Smiths to be able to sell the books on his own in exchange for his financial backing, found that no one wanted the Gold Bible.[42] Joseph even sent out his younger brother Samuel to peddle the book as a traveling salesman, but he had no more luck than Harris.[43] Samuel took seriously Joseph's claims that "the Book of Mormon [was] a record of the forefathers of our western Tribes of Indians," and emphasized that the book was a history of the region and "the origin of the Indians."[44] Even with this stress on the historical nature of the book, New Yorkers shunned the *Book of Mormon* as the worst type of blasphemy. Aside from the fact that its very existence bespoke the inadequacy of the Bible so many Americans held dear, the *Book of Mormon*'s immense thematic and historical complexity did not

Imaginative re-creation of the golden plates placed behind a first edition of the *Book of Mormon*. Photo by Mark Philbrick; courtesy of Neal A. Maxwell Institute for Religious Scholarship, Brigham Young University

enhance the work's appeal. Years later, Mark Twain went so far as to call the book "chloroform in print" because of what he perceived to be its overly repetitive and hopelessly convoluted nature.[45]

Joseph did not apologize for the complexity of his book. After all, one of the Bible's most distinctive features was its complicated nature. The *Book of*

Mormon echoed the Bible not only in this regard, but in its very language and multibook format. Joseph translated the plates in a style of language strangely reminiscent of the English found in the King James Version. Clearly, lines such as "And it came to pass that the Lord spake unto me, saying: Blessed are thou, Nephi, because of thy faith, for thou hast sought me diligently, with lowliness of heart" signaled that the book was not just another newfangled novel or traditional antebellum historical chronicle.[46] Its very language was biblical. The book also echoed the Bible's basic structure. The Protestant Bible, deriving its very name from the Greek words τά βιβλία meaning "the books," contains sixty-six different books in its Old and New Testaments. These books differ widely in terms of genre. Some contain epic histories, while others are composed of biographic, poetic, or prophetic writing. In total, the Bible's narrative covers some four thousand years of ancient history. The structure of the *Book of Mormon* ran in a similar vein. It contained fifteen different books spanning centuries of history, often named after biblical-sounding authors such as Jacob and Alma, and echoed the Bible in its stories of divinely favored people traveling to a promised land, the global importance of the House of Israel, the fulfillment of various sacred prophecies, and the messianic mission of Jesus Christ.[47]

As Joseph explained the origin of his new scripture, he told how Mormon and his son, Moroni, redacted a much larger body of work to create the *Book of Mormon*. This view is critical to an understanding of the book's importance. Mormon and Moroni stood in a long line of prophets, historians, and scribes who reportedly helped write and store thousands of records telling of God's work on the American continent and beyond. Through this great host of record keepers, the *Book of Mormon* taught that each of the tribes that left Palestine kept carefully preserved accounts of God's dealings with them. The *Book of Mormon* hinted at this multiplicity of records when it had God declaring, "For behold, I shall speak unto the Jews, and they shall write it; and I shall also speak unto the Nephites, and they shall write it; and I shall also speak unto the other tribes of the House of Israel, which I have led away, and they shall write it; and I shall also speak unto all the nations of the earth, and they shall write it."[48]

Thus the *Book of Mormon* taught that people over vast expanses of time and space received their own revelations from God. Judea no longer possessed a monopoly on divinely inspired biblical content; throughout the ages, all the world had been filled with sacred revelation. The *Book of Mormon* is just one such divine record, and the Bible simply stood as one of its sister-texts. Furthermore, because of their common, divine origins, the Bible and the *Book of Mormon* testified to each other's veracity. The implication of so many divine records not only pushed the Bible aside as the world's single most important text, but it made the Bible a companion piece to countless other Bible-like records that, while now lost, extended God's message to people in any place and age who might be spiritually attuned to his words.

Joseph positioned himself in this lineage of records and record keepers as God's most recent chosen instrument of grace and redemptive enlightenment. In the final analysis, the *Book of Mormon* could be seen as an analogue to the lever Joseph had first used to move the stone slab to obtain the golden plates hidden below. It pried open the canon of Christian scripture, the set of books contained in the most widely accepted versions of the Bible. To open the canon was to accept that God's revelation did not cease with the apostles of the early Church but continued into the present age, and that additions could be made to the sixty-six books most commonly accepted by Protestants in their version of the Bible.

In the eyes of Joseph's Protestant contemporaries, new books had not been added to the scriptural canon since the fourth century CE. Through the *Book of Mormon*, Joseph sought to change this fact. From these plates, Joseph claimed to have produced a new, equally valid history of God's redemptive work. In fact, he soon went one step further. He claimed that the *Book of Mormon* was a purer text than the Protestant Bible.[49] It had been passed to his hands directly from America's own ancient and inspired scribes, and had not been defiled by centuries of scribal error and Church politics. Along with its more pristine status, the book also testified to the fact that the canon of scripture was not closed. The *Book of Mormon* vividly showed that the Bible was not the only scripture available to those who believed in Christ. A multitude of scriptural accounts existed, of which the Bible and the *Book of Mormon* were only two examples.

In the clearest possible terms, the *Book of Mormon* promised a new era of prophecy and intimate contact with the Divine. Telling anyone who would listen, Joseph proclaimed that God had not only spoken to the ancient Jews of the Middle East; he had spoken to the ancient inhabitants of the Americas. More importantly, Joseph wished those around him to realize that God was still speaking, and in his inscrutable wisdom had chosen Joseph as the Prophet ordained to inaugurate a new biblical age.

Holy Writ or Humbug?

CHAPTER 2

More than sixty years after he set the type for the first edition of the *Book of Mormon*, John Gilbert granted an interview to the *New York Herald* concerning his views on the book and the man who had translated it. Gilbert was not a religious man and never believed that Joseph had found "any plates, unless [he] secured a few of the archaeological plates at a museum to show on extraordinary occasions to doubting friends."[1] He recounted having once met Brigham Young's son, Brigham Young Jr., who asked him whether he thought "our Mormon Bible a humbug."[2] Gilbert replied that he thought it "a very big humbug," a hoax of gigantic proportions.[3] Young then reportedly replied with a smile, "If it is a humbug it is the most successful humbug ever known."[4]

When the *Book of Mormon* first began to circulate in the early 1830s, it entered an incredibly vibrant and increasingly diverse American religious landscape. Joseph's upstate New York was heavily traveled by Methodist circuit riders and revival preachers; historians have come to call it the "Burned-Over District" because the region was so often swept by the flames of the Holy Spirit.[5] Various Protestant denominations vied with each other, as well as with Catholics and new religious traditions such as the Shakers, the followers of the Prophet Matthias, and a growing number of mystical spiritualists, to attract followers to their version of the Gospel message.[6] In looking at this antebellum religious cauldron bubbling with spiritual fervor, one quickly comes to realize that Joseph was just one voice among many proclaiming the birth of a new religious age in America.

Even before the *Book of Mormon* finally emerged from Grandin's press in the spring of 1830, Joseph had begun to reinforce the divine nature of his calling by emphasizing that he was more than a simple translator of an ancient manuscript. He wished to make it clear that he was God's chosen prophet appointed to restore a purer form of Christianity to earth. While translating a section of the manuscript on Jesus's ministry in the Western Hemisphere, Joseph and Oliver Cowdery were struck that among all the country's competing denominations and sects, no one seemed to have clear "authority from

God to administer the ordinances of the gospel."[7] So disturbed were they by this insight that they broke off their translation work and retired to pray near the Susquehanna River. While the two knelt in prayer, John the Baptist appeared to them in angelic form and ordained them into the Priesthood of Aaron, proclaiming that they now had power to baptize "by immersion for the remission of sins."[8] Each man then baptized the other in the river. The angel also promised that later they would be ordained into a higher priesthood, the order of Melchizedek, which would allow them to baptize with the power of the Holy Ghost. Joseph and Cowdery returned to their translation work knowing that the United States was on the verge of not only a new revelation, but also a new divinely appointed authority structure to undergird that revelation's message.

Joseph took seriously his new anointing as an authorized baptizer. Before the first copy of the *Book of Mormon* began to circulate, he organized a new church. On April 6, 1830, he chartered the Church of Christ, a body he renamed, just four years later, the Church of Jesus Christ of Latter-day Saints.[9] Six men lent their names to legalize the new church, while some forty others attended its first service.[10] As his church slowly grew, it drew people who were attracted to its strong claims of authority and its promise of more new revelations. The great draw to his new church was its claim to a unique and privileged status. Joseph offered his followers not only a new word from God, but a restored priestly authority to administer God's sacraments and govern his restored church on earth.

Joseph also attracted followers through his thoroughly democratic and egalitarian message. He decried those who became rich at the cost of the poor around them. With a clearly antiaristocratic bias, Joseph's new church was willing to embrace anyone committed to listening and submitting to God's voice.[11] The lowliest workman or migrant farmer found himself eligible for baptism and then ordination into a ministry of significance. Professional clergy—something the *Book of Mormon* denounced as "priestcraft"—did not exist in Joseph's church.[12] The theme of equality appears constantly throughout the *Book of Mormon*, a fact that is well exemplified by characters such as the Nephite King Benjamin who asks his people: "Are we not all beggars? Do we not all depend upon the same Being, even God, for all the substance which we have?"[13] Joseph built his church upon a firm conviction that all men were created equal, and both men and women flocked to his teaching because it promised that everyone, not just the rich and educated, could enjoy a more intimate relationship with God.[14]

In January 1831, just nine months after the release of the *Book of Mormon*, Joseph decided to move his Church farther out on the nation's western frontier in order to gather his Saints into a single community. It would be the first of three major relocations that Joseph's Church would experience during his lifetime. Initially, he decided to gather his followers at Kirtland, Ohio. Following Kirtland, Joseph moved his Church's central base of operations first to Far West, Missouri, and then to Nauvoo, Illinois. After Joseph's death, Brigham Young moved the Church once again, this time to the Salt Lake Valley of Utah.

Joseph chose Kirtland as his Church's new home because of its proximity to three of the former congregations of Sidney Rigdon, a recent convert and influential Reformed Baptist minister in the region. Charismatic and a singularly powerful preacher, Rigdon led large numbers of his former congregants to embrace Mormonism.[15] Almost overnight, Joseph had a critical mass of believers clustered in northeast Ohio.

Before becoming a Mormon, Rigdon had been a committed follower of Alexander Campbell, a one-time Baptist preacher who taught that the primitive and pure Church found in the pages of the New Testament was attainable in the United States. In the coming years, Campbell spearheaded the cre-

Sidney Rigdon, a onetime Baptist minister and gifted orator, was an important, early convert to Mormonism. Courtesy of the Church Archives, The Church of Jesus Christ of Latter-day Saints

ation of one of the century's most vibrant Protestant denominations, the Disciples of Christ, which numbered some twenty-two thousand adherents in 1832 and grew tenfold by 1860.[16] Rigdon had been one of Campbell's most promising protégés, and his conversion to Mormonism enraged his former mentor. Campbell responded to Rigdon's perfidy by writing the first extended critique of the *Book of Mormon*. The depth of Campbell's anger at Rigdon and the "several hundred persons of different denominations" who had come to believe in Joseph's "romance" is evident throughout his red-hot critical review of the new sacred scripture.[17]

After studying the text, Campbell concluded that Joseph was "as ignorant and impudent a knave as ever wrote a book," a man guided by the composition philosophy that "'the more marvelous the more credible the tale,' and the more fiction the more intelligible and reasonable the narrative."[18] Campbell marveled not only at the book's outrageous story line, but at its factual errors. For Campbell, the depth of Joseph's farce came across clearly when he made such blatant mistakes as identifying Jesus's birthplace as Jerusalem rather than Bethlehem.[19] In the end, Campbell saw Joseph's Gold Bible as little more than a thinly veiled attempt to decide every great controversy that faced American Protestantism in the early nineteenth century, including infant baptism, ordination, the Trinity, regeneration, repentance, church government, and eternal punishment.[20] In a time when Methodists, Presbyterians, Congregationalists, Baptists, and Catholics were all flooding the American frontier with emissaries espousing their different doctrinal points of view, Joseph gained a hearing by cutting through the cacophony of religious disputation with a message that claimed to be a new divine word revealing the true Gospel of Jesus Christ.

Campbell was not alone in his attacks on the young prophet and his book. In the coming years, a considerable host of critics lined up against Joseph. Frequently, those most interested in denouncing Joseph saw discrediting the *Book of Mormon* as the linchpin to destroying his credibility and the truth claims of Mormonism. As the nineteenth century gave way to the twentieth and then twenty-first centuries, three basic lines of argumentation arose to explain, or debunk, the book:

1. The supernaturalist or revelatory school: Joseph had truly received plates and translated a new divine revelation.
2. The plagiarist school: Joseph had plagiarized the book from other sources.
3. The naturalist school: Joseph was simply a gifted storyteller with an amazingly fecund imagination.[21]

Defenders of Joseph's divine calling in the revelatory school rely most heavily on arguments propounding his minimal education. Those who knew Joseph best continually testified that the *Book of Mormon*'s narrative complexity, language, history, and religious content reached far beyond his ability to fabricate. Even Joseph's wife Emma, who had her reasons to be disenchanted with Mormonism (including her husband's later advocacy of polygamy and her extreme distaste for Brigham Young), never doubted that Joseph had indeed translated a set of golden plates. Until the end of her life, she remained absolutely convinced that the book was divinely inspired, telling their son, Joseph Smith III, that his father "could neither write nor dictate a coherent and well-worded letter, let alone dictate a book like the Book of Mormon."[22]

Early, and then later, apologists for the book also hold fast to another reason to trust the book's veracity. There were the three and then the eight witnesses who had actually seen the plates. Although many of these men would later have a checkered history with Joseph and his Church, they never recanted their testimony.[23] The plates themselves may have disappeared, but not before being seen by more men than just the Prophet who translated them.

The plagiarist school finds its origin in the work of Eber D. Howe. In 1834, Howe, a newspaperman in Painesville, Ohio, and a man whose wife, sister, and niece all converted to Mormonism, offered the first book-length attack on Joseph and his new religion. Howe's *Mormonism Unvailed* was based largely on his own critical reading of the *Book of*

Mormon and the testimonies of those with personal knowledge of Joseph and his new Church, such as Phiastus Hurlbut and Ezra Booth. Hurlbut and Booth had been Mormons, but Hurlbut had been excommunicated for immoral behavior and Booth had been expelled for less clear reasons. Both men, however, harbored great enmity toward Joseph and went to considerable lengths to disparage Mormonism and its founder. Hurlbut proved to be the more industrious of the two. He traveled throughout Ohio, New York, and Pennsylvania gathering affidavits from more than sixty individuals bent on proving the dishonorable, lazy, and even vicious propensities of Joseph and his family.[24]

Mormonism Unvailed provided skeptics of the *Book of Mormon* with a series of arguments ranging from its lack of historical accuracy (it had steel in use long before its conventional date of invention and placed horses in the Americas long before their introduction to the region) to the questionable character of its author. One of its most lasting contributions to anti-Mormon literature, however, was that it set forth a rival theory of the book's authorship, claiming that Joseph had stolen and then adjusted the book manuscript of a man named Solomon Spalding (sometimes spelled "Spaulding") to create his supposedly sacred scripture. A Revolutionary War veteran, store owner, and ordained

Congregationalist preacher, Spalding had written a work titled "Manuscript Found," which Spalding's friends claimed bore some striking similarities to Joseph's Gold Bible. Howe actually obtained a copy of "Manuscript Found" from Hurlbut, but he did not find the requisite similarities between the two texts.[25] Instead, Howe introduced the argument in *Mormonism Unvailed* that Joseph and Sidney Rigdon had come across a second Spalding manuscript (now lost) that served as the core text of the *Book of Mormon*.[26]

Howe was not the first to point to Rigdon's role in helping Smith produce the *Book of Mormon*. As early as 1831, people had begun to theorize that the much better educated and more eloquent Rigdon must have been a primary force behind the book's appearance. One widely reprinted newspaper article characterized Rigdon as a man who "had a superior knowledge of human nature, considerable talent, great plausibility, and knew how to work the passion as exactly as a Cape Cod sailor knows how to work a whale ship."[27] In this reporter's opinion, Rigdon was the key "uniting" figure in bringing forth the *Book of Mormon*.[28] Howe believed that Rigdon, who had once lived in Pittsburgh, a place near Spalding's own home, had discovered a Spalding manuscript in a local printing office and had either copied or stolen it. He then worked with Joseph to add a great many biblical passages in order to pass it off as a new scripture translated from non-existent golden plates.

Whether positing the existence of a second Spalding manuscript or some Spalding/Rigdon hybrid creation, the Spalding theory of plagiarism became the single most dominant strain in anti-Mormon apologetics throughout the nineteenth century. The theory allowed non-Mormons to make sense of a basic tension-fraught question: How could a twenty-four-year-old, semiliterate migrant farmer have composed such a long, complicated historical narrative?[29] Scholars agree that Joseph had little formal education, although his father was a schoolteacher for a time and certainly helped teach Joseph what little he knew about reading and writing.[30] Pointing to sources other than Joseph's imagination or a set of golden plates allowed non-Mormons to pose solutions as to how such a poor, ignorant man could have created something as complex as the *Book of Mormon*.

After the nineteenth century, various plagiarism theories lost their preeminent perch as the most favored non-Mormon explanations for the *Book of Mormon*'s origin, but one still occasionally finds them in more modern scholarship on Mormonism. Even though Rigdon maintained throughout his life that he had no knowledge of the book until months after its publication, two more recent groups of scholars have argued for the credibility of Howe's theory that Joseph and Rigdon colluded to create the *Book of Mormon* (1830).[31] In the 1970s, Wayne L. Cowdery (a descendant of Oliver Cowdery) argued through historical evidence and handwriting analysis that Rigdon did have the opportunity to take a now-lost book manuscript of Spalding's and mold it into a new scripture with Joseph's aid.[32] Finding Wayne Cowdery's work "quite plausible," a group of scholars at Stanford University led by Matthew L. Jockers used sophisticated linguistic computer modeling in 2008 to analyze the text of the *Book of Mormon*. Jockers's group concluded: "The *Book of Mormon* was written by multiple, nineteenth-century authors, and more specifically, we find strong support for the Spalding-Ridgon theory of authorship. In all the data, we find Rigdon as a unifying force. His signal dominates the book, and where other candidates are more probable, Rigdon is often hiding in the shadows."[33] This computer analysis took samples of the writings of Solomon Spalding, Sidney Rigdon, Oliver Cowdery, and others to make its judgments, but did not include any writings of Joseph Smith Jr., arguing that no true, verified samples of Joseph's own writing have ever been established. The Stanford group adhered to the belief that Joseph was simply too uneducated to do much, if any, of his own writing.

The naturalist school, propounding that Joseph simply wrote the book, unaided by any plates or divine inspiration, came to prominence in the early twentieth century, ultimately replacing theories of plagiarism as the favored way of explaining the genesis of the *Book of Mormon*. The naturalist school found its most powerful early advocate in the philosopher and religious skeptic Isaac Woodbridge Riley. In his *Founder of Mormonism: A Psychological Study of Joseph Smith, Jr.* (1902), Riley argued that the young prophet had written the work, drawing inspiration from his magic-filled upbringing and other locally available source materials, including Ethan Smith's *View of the Hebrews*.[34] Riley's theory, and others similar to it, held that while Joseph may not have been highly literate, he had an astounding imagination and was a gifted oral storyteller. He may not have been able to write a book, but he was certainly able to dictate one. Joseph's own mother recounted how, long before he sat down to translate the plates, he regaled his family with spellbinding tales of "the ancient inhabitants of this continent, their dress, their manner of traveling, the animals which they rode, the cities that they built, and the structure of their buildings with every particular, their mode of warfare, and their religious worship as specifically as though he had spent his life with them."[35] For those holding to the theory that Joseph was a more ordinary author, it is easy to believe that the stories he supposedly translated from golden plates were but forms of tales he had spent years refining before family and friends.

The naturalist school gained adherents throughout the twentieth century, finding one of its most influential advocates in the historian and university professor Fawn Brodie, perhaps Joseph's most famous—some would say infamous—biographer. In 1945, Brodie published her controversial *No Man Knows My History*. In it, she forcefully argued against the Spalding-Rigdon theory, stating that there existed "no good evidence to show that Rigdon and Smith ever met before Rigdon's conversion late in 1830."[36] Instead, she believed that Joseph was both unusually charismatic and intelligent, fully capable of composing the *Book of Mormon* and enticing others into believing it to be a new revelation from God.[37] According to Brodie, Joseph came to believe his own lies concerning a book he had originally written as a moneymaking hoax. As the years passed, he became ever more convinced that he was indeed God's appointed prophet.[38]

By the turn of the twenty-first century, the naturalist school had divided into two major wings. The first of these is historicist in nature. Its scholars have concentrated on the cultural context in which the book first emerged. Examples of this school include the lay historian David Persuitte and the master bibliographer and book collector Rick Grunder. Both men argue that Joseph was profoundly influenced by early nineteenth-century cultural currents and events, as well as by various texts to which he was exposed. Grunder's *Mormon Parallels* (2008), a remarkable work of more than two thousand pages, is largely bibliographic in nature. He cites hundreds of texts that resonate with the *Book of Mormon*. Grunder includes a wide range of possible intellectual influences on Joseph's narrative of ancient Middle Easterners finding their way to America to become the rootstock of the American Indian.[39]

Persuitte, in his *Joseph Smith and the Origins of "The Book of Mormon"* (2000), exemplifies a school of historical scholarship that seeks to explain Joseph's authorship of the book in a rational, not divinely revelatory, way. According to Persuitte, Joseph "spontaneously dictated" the entire book, masking his own authorship behind certain mystical and magical conventions such as the Urim and Thummim and then a seer stone.[40] Persuitte theorizes that initially Joseph hid behind a blanket with "some notes and books" to aid his dictation, but as the "translation" process progressed, he became ever more comfortable in simply dictating straight from his own imagination (although he might have pinned notes in his hat as he spoke the words his scribe was to write).[41] To explain the testimony of the witnesses, Persuitte speculates that Joseph made a set of tin "dummy plates," which were fully capable of fooling anyone who hefted them in a box or felt them while they were covered by a cloth.[42]

The second wing of the naturalist school has focused its energies on examining the book through a more psychological lens. Leading representatives of this wing include William Morain, Robert Anderson, and Dan Vogel. Morain, a surgeon with a special interest in psychology, came upon the fact that Joseph at age seven had undergone three incredibly painful operations on his leg without anesthesia.[43] Drawing on his intimate knowledge of how surgery affects young patients, Morain argues that Joseph was so psychologically traumatized by these operations—along with the tragic loss of his older brother Alvin—that he developed a psychological condition commonly called "dissociation."[44] This condition enabled Joseph to separate himself from certain painful facets of reality by retreating into an unusually rich fantasy world that eventually expressed itself in the *Book of Mormon*. In Morain's view, Joseph used the composition of the book as a way to process the great traumas of his early life.[45]

Robert Anderson is also a physician; he brings to his study the experience gathered in a long career as a psychiatrist, as suggested by the subtitle of his book, *Inside the Mind of Joseph Smith: Psychobiography and the Book of Mormon*. Anderson sought to "listen" to the 1830 edition *Book of Mormon* in the same way he listened to his patients, creating a "fascinating though not always complimentary" picture of Joseph.[46] Although similar in approach to Morain's study, Anderson's sees Joseph's early surgical traumas as only one part of the puzzle that made up the Prophet's complex psychological profile. Anderson argues that an extreme dissociative disorder did not drive Joseph's composition of the *Book of Mormon*, but instead a personality much more integrated and in control.[47] In the end, Anderson sees Smith as a "narcissistic personality" and the *Book of Mormon* as the creative expression of his grandiose sense of self-importance and appetite for power, uniqueness, and adulation.[48] Arguing that "major psychological conflicts and emotional trauma cannot be totally suppressed in our communications, even with conscious intent," Anderson sees the *Book of Mormon* as a window into Joseph's soul, a work that reveals his feelings about important life events and circumstances: his family's constant displacement and migrations, his upbringing in poverty, or the birth of his stillborn, malformed first child.[49]

Vogel, an independent historian and prolific author on Mormonism, embarks on a related line of psychological argumentation in his biography, *Joseph Smith: The Making of a Prophet* (2004). In this massive tome, he argues that Joseph was a "charlatan" who "came to believe that he was, in fact, called of God and thereafter occasionally used deceit to bolster his religious message."[50] Rather than employing the methods and theories of strict psychoanalysis, Vogel uses a family-systems approach to examine Joseph's life. He explores how various dysfunctional dynamics within Joseph's family provided the building blocks for the Prophet's highly deceptive and delusional behavior as a religious leader, army general, founder of cities, and secret husband to countless wives.[51]

Vogel works systematically through a large cast of important characters in the *Book of Mormon* including King Benjamin, King Mosiah, Nephi, Alma, and Moroni to explore how each one reflected Joseph's deepest passions and anxieties. Mosiah, for example, "mirrored Joseph's role as translator," a king who had a prophetic gift that enabled him to translate unknown languages.[52] For Vogel, the connection between Mosiah and Smith becomes even more striking when one considers how, during his reign, Mosiah sent out an expedition to find a group that had disappeared while attempting to return to the ancient land of Nephi. Mosiah's expedition finds remnants of this group, now under the leadership of the Nephite King Limhi. Limhi's people, however, are currently in bondage to the Lamanite King Laman, who works them hard and taxes them heavily. Limhi wishes to return with his people to Mosiah's land and finally is able to escape from Laman with his people.[53]

For Vogel, Limhi's situation "subtlety [*sic*] parallels Joseph Smith's situation in Harmony" after his marriage to Emma Hale.[54] Emma had longed to return to Harmony, and Vogel parallels Emma's desire with Limhi's situation under the oppressive rule of King Laman. When Joseph and Emma did return to the Hale homestead, they found themselves under the tyrannical hand of Emma's father, Isaac, who had little patience for Joseph's prophetic aspirations and demanded that he find suitable, earthly work to support himself and his young bride. Despising his life under Isaac Hale's disapproving eye, Joseph used Limhi's story to teach Emma that it was better to live "in freedom in a foreign land than in bondage in one's homeland."[55] In such a manner, Vogel interprets countless stories in the *Book of Mormon* as autobiographical windows into Joseph's life challenges and complicated mind.[56]

Although theories abound that seek to explain the *Book of Mormon* as a human creation, the fact remains that in the nearly two centuries since the book's appearance, it has attracted millions of adherents. To some degree, whether the book is a humbug or not is a moot question. Millions today believe it to be Holy Writ. Part of the book's influence may be attributed to its content, but it is a work that cannot be fully appreciated outside its close relationship to its supposed prophet and translator. To understand the magnetic power of the *Book of Mormon*, one must seek to understand the life, and particularly the prophetic role, of the man who brought it forth.

Budding

PART II

But behold, it shall come to pass that they
shall be driven and scattered by the Gentiles;
and . . . then will the Lord remember
the covenant which he made unto Abraham
and unto all the house of Israel.

—Mormon 5:20

Multiplying Prophets

While controversy surrounded the *Book of Mormon* from its inception, the fact remained that perhaps the book's greatest attraction was how it provided the ever-growing number of Mormon converts a tangible testimony that God was once again speaking to humanity. Absolutely central to any understanding of the religious power and influence of the book is the prophetic figure who ushered it into the world. The book and the Prophet functioned in a symbiotic relationship of mutual credentialing. The presence of a new sacred text testified to the special status and powers of Joseph, who had translated it, and in turn Joseph testified to the truth of the book through his continuing revelations from God. Neither the Prophet nor the book would, without the other, wield the oracular power each enjoyed.

Joseph embraced his divinely anointed prophetic appointment when he moved to Kirtland,

Ohio, in 1831, going so far as to introduce himself to others as "Joseph the prophet."[1] The book showed him to be a man set apart by God for a special purpose, and he continued to show just how special he was by continuing to receive new messages directly from God. In Kirtland, God spoke to him on a wide range of topics, including how to administer the sacraments properly (using water instead of wine for communion), guidelines for missionary activity, and where the Church should establish its next outposts. Eventually Joseph received so many revelations that it was considered prudent to gather them all in one place. In 1833, the Church published the *Book of Commandments*, a compendium of sixty-five revelations Joseph had received up through September 1831.[2]

Other revelatory works would follow, including a revised and expanded edition of the *Book of Commandments* entitled *Doctrine and Covenants* (1835) and *The Pearl of Great Price* (1851).[3] Joseph's gifts of translation and prophecy also manifested themselves in his continued work on revising various sections of the Bible.[4] For the most part, Joseph only made subtle changes to the biblical text, adjusting it to align more readily with his own theology on such issues as predestination and baptism, but he did add some longer sections to the Bible as well, including additions to the Gospel of Matthew that helped explain in greater detail the critical events of Christ's Second Coming and the Final Judgment. Even though Joseph's revised Bible was not published during his lifetime, many of his longer additions to the biblical text did circulate and eventually came to be included in *The Pearl of Great Price*. For most Mormons, Joseph's published revelations in the *Doctrine and Covenants* and *The Pearl of Great Price* attained a status by the end of the nineteenth century that placed these two works alongside the Bible and the *Book of Mormon* as the canonical, sacred texts of Mormonism.

In the years following the founding of the Church, Joseph embraced other revelatory work of an even more startling nature. He returned to the *Book of Mormon* twice to revise its text. In Joseph's hands, the *Book of Mormon* was no static entity. A living prophet made it a living book, capable of change. His oracular status made him fully comfortable in correcting what he told his followers was "the most correct of any book on earth."[5]

He first revised the book in 1837. This second edition proved important because it included more than three thousand alterations from the 1830 edition, clearly signaling that the Prophet was not afraid to change his work.[6] For the most part, these changes were matters of adjustments in grammar. Examples include "which" being changed to "who" over seven hundred times, and "saith" being altered to "said" over two hundred times.[7] Joseph had, however, made theological adjustments to the text as well, hoping to rid the book of inconsistencies and harmonize its content with his more recent teachings found in "Lectures on the Faith" and the 1835 edition of the *Doctrine and Covenants*.[8] The most important changes in this regard appear in the first two books of Nephi where Joseph revised to indicate a difference in the person of the Godhead, making way for his further teachings on the plurality of gods. For example, Joseph changed his wording in 1 Nephi 14:30 from "the Lamb of God is the Eternal Father and Savior of the world" to "the Lamb of God is the *Son of the* Eternal Father and the Savior of the world" (italics added).[9] Joseph made only a dozen or so theological changes to the book, and most of them occur early on in the text. One wonders whether his revelations were limited to these early sections, or time constraints or faltering interest kept him from further revisions.

A third edition of the *Book of Mormon* appeared in 1840.[10] It was the last edition of the book to include new revisions by Joseph himself. For the third edition, Joseph worked with the printer, Ebenezer Robinson, to compare the 1830 and 1837 editions, along with the manuscripts from which the 1830 edition was set, to uncover and correct errors.[11] As with the second edition, most of the corrections were grammatical, but on a few occasions Joseph added explanation or changed wording. For example, in 1 Nephi 20:1, after "out of the waters of Judah" he added the parenthetical phrase "(or out of the waters of baptism)."[12] Carefully reviewing the book's entire text, Joseph made roughly forty-seven changes.

As Joseph continued to receive revelations, his Church slowly spread deeper into America's western frontier. Joseph himself relocated in the spring of 1838 to Caldwell County, Missouri. Because of persecution by neighboring non-Mormons, he moved again within months to Commerce, Illinois, a town he renamed "Nauvoo" from the Hebrew meaning "beauty or repose."[13] By 1845, with some eleven thousand residents, Nauvoo had grown to rival Chicago as one of the state's two largest cities.[14] Joseph carefully planned every aspect of Nauvoo, including the building of a grand three-story hotel called the Nauvoo House. When this building's cornerstone was laid on April 6, 1841 (eleven years to the day after the Church's founding), Joseph ran home to get the handwritten manuscript used to produce the *Book of Mormon*. He returned with the large stack of papers and placed them inside the building's cornerstone, reportedly saying, "I have had trouble enough with this thing."[15] The manuscript would be recovered years later badly damaged by water that had seeped into the stone compartment.[16]

As Joseph established their new Zion in Illinois, his neighbors once again grew uneasy with his political power. His creation of a formidable militia called the Nauvoo Legion did not allay their fears. Matters were further complicated by his increasingly unorthodox revelations. Some scholars have noted that had Mormonism adhered to the teachings found in the *Book of Mormon*, it would have differed little on central doctrinal issues from the country's other Protestant denominations.[17] The *Book of Mormon* is Trinitarian in nature and a strong proponent of monogamy; it contains none of the more aggressive revelations about the plurality of gods and marrying more than one woman that came to mark Mormonism in the later part of Joseph's life.[18] Without these doctrines, non-Mormons might have had less cause to attack the religion and its adherents.

Perhaps no new revelation announced by Joseph was more contentious than his teaching on polygamy, something known within the Church as "plural marriage." Joseph may have toyed with the idea of plural marriage as early as 1831, but he did not officially credential the practice as a sacrament until he was "sealed" to an additional wife, Louisa

Beaman, in April 1841.[19] Even with his marriage to Beaman, Joseph continued to keep the practice a closely guarded secret, revealing it only to his closest confidants.[20] Although the Church recorded a revelation touching on the issue of plural marriage in 1843, Joseph never publically advocated polygamy, and the practice of plural marriages did not become public until 1852, after the Saints had safely established themselves in Utah.[21] This secrecy, however, did not stop Joseph from marrying more than thirty women.[22] Other top Church leaders followed Joseph's example. By the time Brigham Young, Joseph's successor, led the Saints on their momentous trek to Utah in 1847, he had twelve wives and at least nine children.[23]

Although polygamy may have been the most socially unsettling of Joseph's revelations, it was not his only distinct teaching. New doctrinal revelations abounded. Joseph instituted a sacramental ritual for baptizing the dead, and at the funeral of a man named King Follet around the time of the Church's 1844 Annual Conference, he preached what became known as his "King Follett Discourse," in which he made the startling proclamation that there existed a vast plurality of gods, all of whom had once been human.[24] Joseph then encouraged his listeners to strive for their own eventual godhood.[25] By the early 1840s, Joseph had set off in a significantly new direction from orthodox Christian teaching.

Many of his followers began to question these doctrinal innovations and the prophet from whom they came.[26] Dissident Mormons decided to begin publishing a periodical, the *Nauvoo Expositor*, to shine a spotlight on Joseph's heterodox teachings and attack the reputations and practices of prominent Mormon leaders. Only one issue was ever published, as Joseph quickly suppressed the newspaper and destroyed the printing press that had produced it. The action was ill-considered, however, as it further inflamed non-Mormon opposition in the area. The neighboring town of Carthage mobilized its militia and arrested Joseph for disturbing the peace, a charge that eventually transformed into one of treason. Then disaster struck. A vigilante band attacked the Carthage jail where Joseph and his brother Hyrum were imprisoned. The band killed both men. In the blink of an eye, the Church lost its founder and its most direct link to God.

An unprecedented crisis now confronted the Latter-day Saints. The only leader their Church had ever known was dead. As the shock of Joseph's death reverberated throughout Nauvoo, mourning soon gave way to a titanic struggle for control of the Church. The Church splintered as various aspirants attempted to claim the Prophet's mantle of leadership. In the months and years to come, Brighamites, Josephites, Rigdonites, Bickertonites, Strangites, Reorganites, and numerous others vied to become the most legitimate branch of the post-Joseph Mormon Church. Since Joseph's death in 1844, there have arisen some seventy different Mormon sects, nearly fifty of which still exist today (most are quite small).[27] Inevitably, each of these sects developed its own special relationship to the *Book of Mormon*.

Before his death, Joseph had left no clear instructions about who his successor might be. Matters were complicated by the fact that arguably the highest-ranking official after Joseph was Sidney Rigdon, a man whom Joseph had attempted to remove from his position as a member of the Church's highest level of leadership, the First Presidency, but Rigdon's popular support allowed him to retain his post. Rigdon, however, had not followed Joseph to Nauvoo. Instead he had moved to Pittsburgh, Pennsylvania, and while he made a number of extended visits to Nauvoo, he never called the city his home. Upon hearing of Joseph's death, however, Rigdon hastily made his way to Illinois. He entered Nauvoo with every intention of taking Joseph's leadership mantle upon himself. The Church leaders in Nauvoo had different plans.

On a hot August morning, just weeks after Joseph's death, the Church leaders called the Saints together in a huge field to determine who their next leader would be. Both Rigdon and Brigham Young, the president of the Quorum of the Twelve Apostles (the highest ruling body after the Church's president and his counselors), were slated to address the crowd. By every account, Rigdon gave a disappointing, wandering, and uninspiring speech, but when Young took his place atop the bed of an open wagon, he transfixed the crowd.[28] Legend has it that a miraculous event occurred when he addressed the Saints. As he spoke, his listeners marveled that "not only was it the voice of Joseph which was heard, but...it was the very person of Joseph which stood before them."[29] The crowd quickly and overwhelmingly rallied to Young, who, although he did not claim the role of prophet (a position he said only God could bestow), assured those present that Joseph had indeed given the Quorum of the Twelve, which Young led, "the keys of the kingdom of God in all the world" to "manage the affairs of the church and direct all things aright."[30] In the ensuing vote, the Saints overwhelmingly affirmed Brigham Young and the Quorum of the Twelve as the new leaders of the Church.[31]

Although the vote decisively favored Young, the struggle for control of the Church was only beginning. Rigdon protested his defeat, saying that Young had acted without the proper authority to override

Brigham Young succeeded Joseph Smith Jr. as the leader of the Church of Jesus Christ of Latter-day Saints and was instrumental in the mass Mormon migration to Utah. Courtesy of the Church Archives, The Church of Jesus Christ of Latter-day Saints

the power of the First Presidency. Young quickly lost patience with Rigdon and excommunicated him. Rigdon retaliated by excommunicating Young and the entire Quorum of the Twelve Apostles.

Rigdon soon left Nauvoo, and returned to Pitts-burgh to lead his own Mormon faction, a group that became commonly known as the Rigdonites. By 1847, internal dissensions decimated Rigdon's following. Only when William Bickerton took control of the few remaining Rigdonites did this faction of Mormonism achieve some measure of stability. Bickerton reorganized the Rigdonites in 1862 under the name the Church of Jesus Christ. For a time they flourished in eastern Pennsylvania, becoming known among their neighbors and other Mormons by the sobriquet "Bickertonites."[32] Rig-don's and Bickerton's followers revered the Bible and the *Book of Mormon*, but did not canonize the *Doctrine and Covenants* or *The Pearl of Great Price*, disbelieving many of Joseph's later revelations. This wing of Mormonism still exists today with some twelve thousand members worldwide.[33]

While Rigdon may have been the highest-ranking Mormon to lay claim to Joseph's leadership position, he was not the man who ultimately most seriously challenged Brigham Young for the reins of the Mormon church. James Strang, a Mormon missionary to Wisconsin, earned that honor. Strang had been baptized by Joseph himself, and upon hearing of the Prophet's death, he produced a "Let-ter of Appointment" supposedly written by Joseph and bearing a Nauvoo postmark dated just eleven

James Strang was the most successful of the early challeng-
ers to Brigham Young's authority in the Church. Courtesy
of the Church Archives, The Church of Jesus Christ of
Latter-day Saints

days before the tragic events in Carthage. The letter's authenticity would be much contested in the
months to follow, but the document served Strang's
purposes well.[34] It stated without equivocation that

Joseph had appointed Strang to succeed him as the Church's leader and prophet. Adding to this letter's testimony, Strang claimed that after Joseph's death he had been visited by an angel, who had appointed him to take the Prophet's place. Young decried Strang's claims as delusional and promptly excommunicated him and any Saint who joined him.

Others did not dismiss Strang so quickly. Strang claimed certain credentials to lead the Church that Young did not. Strang not only produced his "Letter of Appointment," but he represented himself as a prophet and translator just as Joseph had. Following Joseph's own script, Strang bolstered his leadership claim by saying that he had been visited by an angel who had revealed a new set of plates to be translated. Strang made the news of this angelic vision as public as possible among the Saints, arguing that Young and his cohort had never claimed prophetic powers and that the Church always had been—and needed to be—led by a prophet.

To legitimize his claim to succession, Strang unearthed the plates in the presence of witnesses, thereby performing before an audience the all-too-obvious parallels he was drawing between his calling and Mormonism's fallen prophet.[35] And, just like Joseph, he used the book that he eventually translated from these plates to testify to his divinely ordained role as both a translator and a prophet. Strang followed this first sacred revelation (*Voree Plates*, 1845) with another text (*Book of the Law of the Lord*, 1851), which he claimed was translated from the very Plates of Laban mentioned in the *Book of Mormon*. In recovering ancient plates and then translating them, Strang was re-creating the powerful credentialing dynamic Joseph himself had used to have a prophet and a sacred record testify to one another. In this way, his *Voree Plates* and *Book of the Law* became just as important to his sect as was the *Book of Mormon*. Through his claims to being an active prophet and translator of sacred records, Strang attracted thousands of followers, many of whom migrated first to join him in Voree, Wisconsin, and then later at Beaver Island in Lake Michigan. By 1856, his church had grown to around twelve thousand members, nearly two-thirds the number of Mormons located in Utah under Young's leadership at the time.[36]

In a career that manifested numerous intended and unintended resonances with Joseph's own life, Strang came to exercise almost total control over his followers and the doctrines that defined his brand of Mormonism. His visions of grandeur and his controlling style of leadership led to the disaffection of many of his followers. In 1856, two former members of his flock shot him in the back, inflicting wounds that would eventually kill him, three weeks later. With its prophet dead, the Strangite Church spiraled into a decline from which it would never recover.

While the Strangite wing of the Church withered upon its prophet's death, there still existed numerous other rival Mormon factions. The year following his brother's death, William Smith attempted to gather his own following, teaching that Joseph had intended the Church's leadership to be patrilineal, "as set forth in the revelation, from father to son, and hence the eldest son should succeed the father."[37] William proclaimed that someone of Joseph's family, most likely his oldest son, should succeed the fallen prophet. The problem was that Joseph Smith III was but eleven when his father died.[38] Because Joseph Smith III was so young, William appointed himself as a trustee to govern the Church until Joseph's son was old enough to assume his rightful place as the Church's leader. William Smith never gained a large following, but his emphasis on patrilineal descent would become important to another, much more prosperous, group of Saints who colloquially were known as "Josephites" because of their commitment to patrilineal leadership. Later this group took the name Reorganized Church of Latter Day Saints (RLDS).[39] After their formal incorporation as a new Mormon Church, many began to call them "Reorganites."[40]

The RLDS began as a loose confederation of Mormons most often defined by two common characteristics: their opposition to polygamy and their unhappiness with the leadership of Brigham Young. Beginning in 1850, convinced that "neither J. J. Strang, B. Young, William Smith, nor any that had claimed to be prophets, since Joseph's death were the servants of God," this group began holding conferences where they maintained that the leader of the Church should be one of the fallen prophet's blood relations.[41] They were convinced that the Church itself had been corrupted since 1833 when it had both strayed from its founding tenets and renamed itself the Church of Jesus Christ of Latter-day Saints. This group wished to return to the Church's "Community of Christ" days, and held in esteem the Bible, the *Book of Mormon*, Joseph's translation of the Bible, and the *Book of Commandments*. The group was far slower to embrace Joseph's later revelations. Ultimately its leaders would create their own distinct version of the *Doctrine and Covenants*.

Jason W. Briggs became a pivotal figure in the early organization of the RLDS movement. After Joseph's death, Briggs moved from one Mormon faction to another. At first he supported Young, then Strang, and then William Smith. By the early 1850s, he became convinced that no clear leader had arisen to replace the fallen prophet, and after seek-

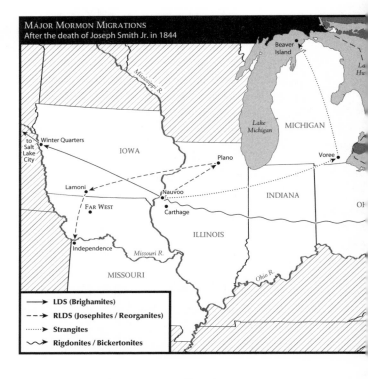

Beaver Island

Mississippi R.

La
Hu

Lake
Michigan   MICHIGAN

to
Salt
Lake
City   Winter Quarters

IOWA

Plano

Voree

Lamoni

Nauvoo

INDIANA

Far West

Carthage

OH

Independence

Missouri R.

ILLINOIS

Ohio R.

MISSOURI

→   LDS (Brighamites)

- - →   RLDS (Josephites / Reorganites)

····→   Strangites

〰   Rigdonites / Bickertonites

ing divine guidance through prayer, he was certain that the Church's leadership was to pass to someone of Joseph's "seed."[42] Briggs then initiated a series of meetings with various midwestern Mormon congregations to bind together until they could once again be headed by one of Joseph's descendants. Briggs functioned as the "presiding officer"—and ultimately as the president of a new Quorum of the Twelve—of these Saints during the earliest period

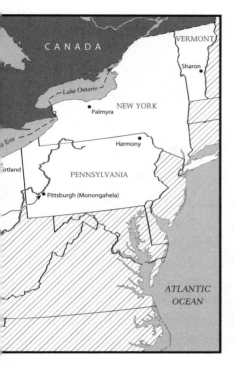

As Mormonism splintered after Joseph Smith Jr.'s death in 1844, different sects settled in various parts of the nation and fostered their own unique relationships to the *Book of Mormon*. Courtesy of the Church Archives, The Church of Jesus Christ of Latter-day Saints

of the consolidation and reorganization that would eventually emerge as the RLDS Church.[43]

Throughout the 1850s, Briggs and others who came to compose the RLDS Church reached out to Joseph Smith III in an attempt to woo him to take his place as their leader. After a great deal of soul-searching and prayer, Joseph Smith III, at the age of twenty-seven, finally accepted the presidency of the RLDS Church. It was a position he would hold for

Joseph Smith III, the eldest surviving son of Joseph Smith Jr., became the first prophet-president of the Reorganized Church of Latter Day Saints. Courtesy of the Church Archives, The Church of Jesus Christ of Latter-day Saints

the next fifty-four years. On April 6, 1860 (thirty years to the day after Joseph first organized his Church), he officially stepped into his new leadership role.

Inevitably, the RLDS came to define itself against the Mormon Church in Utah.[44] Locating its headquarters first in Plano, Illinois; then in Lamoni, Iowa; and finally in Independence, Missouri, the Reorganized Saints represented themselves as the purer church, untainted by the mistakes practiced by the "Saints" in Utah. The RLDS's strong position against polygamy was just one doctrinal issue that separated it from the Utah Church. By 1878, the Reorganites had rejected Joseph's doctrine on the plurality of gods.[45] As the RLDS Church renounced various theological positions adhered to by the Utah Mormons, it embraced more traditional Protestant notions on issues such as heaven, baptism, and the Trinity. In time, certain temple rituals introduced in Joseph's final years also fell by the wayside, including practices associated with baptizing the dead and eternal marriage.[46]

As the RLDS Church moved away from some of Joseph's later, more controversial teachings, it also eschewed several works embraced as canonical scripture among the Utah Mormons. For example, while the Utah Mormons had come to accept *The Pearl of Great Price* as a sacred text, the RLDS Church moved away from the book because it advanced positions with which they did not agree, such as a strong advocacy of the plurality of gods doctrine. Instead, the RLDS Church emphasized the importance of the *Book of Mormon* and Joseph's retranslation of the Bible.[47] In this spirit, the RLDS

Church published the first edition of Joseph's retranslation of the Bible in 1867.

From its earliest days, the RLDS Church revered three texts in its scriptural canon: the Bible,
the *Book of Mormon*, and its version of the *Doctrine
and Covenants*. Although the RLDS Church had
printed editions of the *Book of Mormon* as early
as 1874, it was only decades later that the RLDS
Church produced its own corrected version of the
Book of Mormon. Guided by an editorial committee that compared the 1837 Kirtland edition to the
original printer's manuscript, which had been ac-
quired by the RLDS Church, the committee also
added its own system of notes and versification to
produce what it considered the definitive edition
of the *Book of Mormon*.[48] When it was completed
in 1908, the editors proudly anointed their edition
the "Authorized Version." The RLDS Church also
published its own version of the *Doctrine and Covenants* beginning in 1864. As time passed, this *Doctrine and Covenants* increasingly marked out the
differences between the RLDS and LDS branches
of Mormonism.

What is striking about the RLDS Church, however, is that although it began as a restoration of a
restorationist church movement intent on return-
ing Mormonism to the earliest, purest teachings
of Joseph Smith, as time passed, it proved itself

freer than its LDS Utah counterpart to adapt and change the text of the *Book of Mormon*. For example, in 1966, the Reorganized Saints published the New Authorized Version (or "reader's edition") of the *Book of Mormon*, the first attempt to modernize the book and its language. The New Authorized Version offered its readers a simpler, more straightforward text. It removed archaic words like "durst," "wroth," and the "thee"s and "thou"s, as well as the "th" endings from many of the book's verbs: "supposeth" became "suppose," for example, and "oweth" became "owe." It also standardized punctuation and removed more than one thousand iterations of "and it came to pass." In the end, it was a version intended to clarify the basic message of the book, but its popularity was limited among Mormon readers.[49]

Such permissiveness reached new heights at the turn of the twenty-first century when the president of the RLDS Church, W. Grant McMurray, declared that the modern scholarly scrutiny brought to bear on the *Book of Mormon* had shown the book to fall "outside the traditional standards of historical documentation and veracity."[50] McMurray opened the door to considering the book more myth than history. Distancing itself from its much larger LDS cousin, the RLDS Church not only moved away from treating the *Book of Mormon* as an absolutely historical text, but, beginning in the 1960s, it made a series of concerted moves to define itself not as "the one true church of Jesus Christ on earth" but instead "as one manifestation of the whole body of believers in Christ."[51] Uniqueness gave way to ecumenicalism.[52]

By the closing decades of the twentieth century, the RLDS Church increasingly embraced doctrinal positions and practices that had already gained popularity among American mainline Protestant denominations. The Church ordained women to its priesthood in 1984, moved to define itself by its pronounced interest in social concerns (especially its interest in promoting world peace), opened its communion (offering the sacrament to non-RLDS people), and began to stress less literalist readings of scripture, including the *Book of Mormon*.[53] In 2001 as a reflection of its movement toward ecumenicalism, the RLDS Church abandoned its "Latter Day Saint" designation as it renamed itself "The Community of Christ."[54] The RLDS Church wished others to see it not as a faction of Mormonism, but as a body of believers aligned with Christians from around the world. Today, the Community of Christ remains the second-largest Mormon-founded group, with approximately 250,000 members worldwide as compared to the Utah branch of Mormonism (LDS), which numbers near 14 million. Many of its members still revere the *Book of Mormon*, but the Church does not exalt the book in the way Mormonism's founding prophet had. By the twenty-first century, the newly named Community of Christ had definitely taken some of the shine off Joseph's Gold Bible.

Great Basin Saints and the Book

CHAPTER 4

While Mormonism splintered in the wake of Joseph's death, Brigham Young worked heroically to not only keep the Church of Jesus Christ of Latter-day Saints (LDS) together, but give it a vision for its future. Most immediately, that future involved moving the Saints westward so that they might be able to practice their religion without the fear of persecution from either their neighbors or the government. The need was particularly urgent because by 1845 non-Mormons neighboring Nauvoo made it clear that the Saints must move, threatening military action if they did not leave the state. They disliked the Mormon practice of block voting, their threatening militia, and the rising rumors of polygamy. Just weeks before his death, Joseph had encouraged his leaders to "[b]e ready to start for the Great Basin in the Rocky Mountains."[1] Young took Joseph's words seriously. By the summer of 1847, the first Mormon settlers were arriving in this "Great Basin," the valley region surrounding Utah's Great Salt Lake.

The Great Basin was a vast, unsettled area outside any effective national governmental control.[2] An often forbidding area full of mountains and deserts, it did contain numerous rivers flowing into the Great Salt Lake that were robust enough to support large agricultural communities. By the early 1850s, twenty thousand Mormons had established several new cities in the Great Basin, including Salt Lake City, Ogden, Manti, and Provo. The area became the epicenter for Mormonism as it provided a location isolated enough to allow Brigham Young the freedom to build his Church both doctrinally and communally. Even today with LDS membership numbering nearly fourteen million, the Church's leadership and primary administrative offices are still located in Salt Lake City, and Utah remains the densest population locus for Mormonism in the world.[3]

The same persecutions that drove the Mormons to Utah had a profound impact on the publishing history of the *Book of Mormon*. The numerous moves by the Saints, culminating in the exodus from Nauvoo in the mid-1840s, so destabilized the Church's institutional printing practices that its publishing activities in England became ever more important. For a quarter century after Joseph's death, the LDS Church relied primarily on the Saints in England to publish, store, and distribute the majority of its printed materials aside from periodicals.[4]

The first European edition of the *Book of Mormon* was produced in Liverpool in 1841 by missionaries who found the British interest in Mormonism intense enough to warrant publishing an edition of the book on that side of the Atlantic.[5] To appreciate fully the importance of the 1841 European edition, one must first understand the bibliographic pedigree of the book. The 1841 edition was based on the 1837 second edition, not Joseph's final revised third edition of 1840. The English missionaries had departed before Joseph had created the third edition, a fact with long-lasting consequences. It meant that British editors would base all their editions on a text that did not include Joseph's final revisions.

As the Church's publishing enterprises consolidated in England, British Church leaders became highly important custodians and arbiters of the *Book of Mormon* text. They made changes in the formatting of the book that lasted for decades. For example, in the 1841 Liverpool edition an index appeared for the first time in the form of an extensive table of contents, organized according to the order of the text. This index would appear in every subsequent edition up to the revision of 1920. The third European edition of 1852 also contained important formatting changes. This edition's primary editor, Franklin D. Richards, worked diligently to correct the grammatical and printing errors of the two earlier European editions.[6] He also introduced chapter markers in the running titles and numbered paragraphs throughout the text to facilitate cross-referencing.[7] Stereotype plates were used to print the 1852 edition, and their importance cannot be overstated, as they became the plates from which all subsequent impressions of the book were made until the Church published a new revision in 1879.[8]

Ultimately, the importance of the European editions of the *Book of Mormon* is seen in how they became the rootstock for all later editions up through 1981, when the Church produced a new edition collated from the manuscripts used to print the 1830 edition, as well as the text of the European editions and the last revisions Joseph had made in the 1840 edition. The 1981 became the most bibliographically comprehensive edition of the book ever produced by the Church. It stands as a landmark edition, the most recent and most scholarly textual revision of the *Book of Mormon*, and the edition that the LDS Church still uses today.[9]

It is by considering the American and British lines of *Book of Mormon* bibliographic tradition that one is able to make sense of the highly controversial change in the wording of 2 Nephi 30:6 in the 1981 edition of the book. In the 1830 version of the

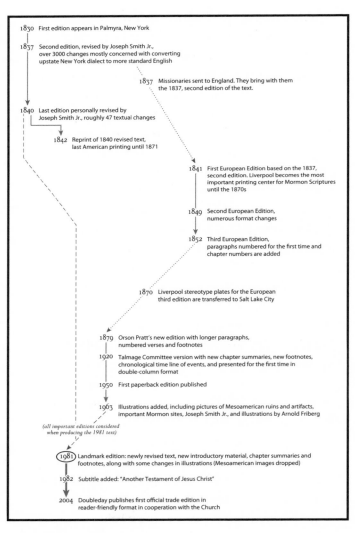

1830 First edition appears in Palmyra, New York

1837 Second edition, revised by Joseph Smith Jr.,
      over 3000 changes mostly concerned with converting
      upstate New York dialect to more standard English

1837 Missionaries sent to England. They bring with them
      the 1837, second edition of the text.

1840 Last edition personally revised by
      Joseph Smith Jr., roughly 47 textual changes

1842 Reprint of 1840 revised text,
      last American printing until 1871

1841 First European Edition based on the 1837,
      second edition. Liverpool becomes the most
      important printing center for Mormon Scriptures
      until the 1870s

1849 Second European Edition,
      numerous format changes

1852 Third European Edition,
      paragraphs numbered for the first time and
      chapter numbers are added

1870 Liverpool stereotype plates for the European
      third edition are transferred to Salt Lake City

1879 Orson Pratt's new edition with longer paragraphs,
      numbered verses and footnotes

1920 Talmage Committee version with new chapter summaries, new footnotes,
      chronological time line of events, and presented for the first time in
      double-column format

1950 First paperback edition published

1963 Illustrations added, including pictures of Mesoamerican ruins and artifacts,
      important Mormon sites, Joseph Smith Jr., and illustrations by Arnold Friberg

*(all important editions considered
when producing the 1981 text)*

1981 Landmark edition: newly revised text, new introductory material, chapter summaries and
      footnotes, along with some changes in illustrations (Mesoamerican images dropped)

1982 Subtitle added: "Another Testament of Jesus Christ"

2004 Doubleday publishes first official trade edition in
      reader-friendly format in cooperation with the Church

Important LDS editions.

text, this verse had read, "And their scales of darkness shall begin to fall from their eyes: and many generations shall not pass away among them, save they shall be a white and delightsome people."[10] In the 1840 version, Joseph changed the wording to read "pure and delightsome." The editors of the 1981 version chose to include the wording of Joseph's last revision. Heated debate ensued as non-Mormons attacked the fickleness of the Church, claiming that its 1978 doctrinal change to allow those with dark skin into the priesthood necessitated this adjustment. Critics claimed that the LDS Church simply changed its scripture whenever it needed to accommodate new doctrinal precepts.[11] Such textual fluidity was certainly not new to Mormonism. Joseph had felt free to make changes in the second and third editions of the text. The Church did not defend the choice, however, on these grounds, but argued that the 1840 edition gave them ample justification for the change. After all, "pure and delightsome" was the Prophet's last version of this verse.

In the 1870s, Mormon leaders finally felt that the publishing resources in the Great Basin had developed enough to enable the Church to centralize its printing enterprises in Salt Lake City. They brought the stereotype plates for the *Book of Mormon* from England to Utah sometime around 1870, allowing Church leaders in Utah to exercise greater oversight of the book's production.[12] One Church leader in particular, a man by the name of Orson Pratt, took advantage of this dawning of a new age of Mormon publishing to produce an incredibly important revised edition of the *Book of Mormon* in 1879.

At the age of nineteen, Pratt had been one of Joseph's first converts; he remained a committed member until his death in 1881. By 1835 he had already served on several missions and was named to the original Quorum of the Twelve Apostles. He held various important leadership roles within the Church throughout his life. He also became a true believer in the rising power of print in the United States. As a wide range of printed material began to become ever more available and influential among antebellum Americans, Pratt helped to spearhead the Church's earliest efforts in pamphleteering.

Among Pratt's most important efforts in authorship and publishing are six tracts defending the *Book of Mormon*, which came to be grouped under the heading *Divine Authenticity of the Book of Mormon* (1850–1852).[13] This set of tracts offered lines of apologetic reasoning that are still used by the LDS Church today.[14] Pratt centered his defense of the book on the fundamental belief that God still spoke to his creation. He spoke to believers personally, through present-day prophets, and through new sacred revelations. Pratt decried how the "whole of

Christendom" quarreled about the Bible, a book that was an "insufficient guide" because it had been so "awfully corrupted" by men.[15] In the *Book of Mormon*, humanity had been given a purer testament and one that stood as a vivid witness that God wished to restore his true Church to the earth.

Pratt's *Divine Authenticity* helped establish him as the Church's greatest apologist for the book after Joseph's death. He was widely respected, if not universally beloved in the Mormon community, as a missionary, educator, theologian, and scientist. His knowledge of printing combined with his encyclopedic knowledge of the text—he claimed to have read it "more carefully than any other man that has ever lived"—made him the perfect person to offer the Church its first great revision of the text since 1840.[16] He was no novice when it came to publishing the *Book of Mormon*. President of the British Mission, he was the guiding hand behind the second European edition of 1849, and as such this edition's title page bears his name.[17] He also was the force behind perhaps one of the most intriguing editions of the *Book of Mormon*, a text printed in the phonetic Deseret Alphabet developed for use in the Utah territory. Pratt transliterated the text into the Deseret Alphabet and saw the edition published in 1869.[18]

Pratt was in the final decade of his seventy-year life when he turned his attention to his grand revision of

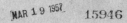

The phonetic Deseret Alphabet was invented in the Utah territory by George Watt around 1854. Endorsed by Brigham Young, the alphabet was intended to provide immigrants with an easier way to learn English and gain access to Mormonism's founding text. Courtesy of the Church Archives, The Church of Jesus Christ of Latter-day Saints the *Book of Mormon*. He wished his edition to be a lasting monument to the book that had so influenced his own life. In this spirit, he worked in his usual systematic and scientific way to carefully compare past editions to remove printing errors. He also worked hard to provide a new detailed, carefully organized apparatus to the text, including an extended table of contents, internal cross-references at the bottom of each page, and new chapter and verse markings. He added to the text roughly seventy-five informative geographic footnotes directly linking events in the narrative to specific locations. He told his readers that the "promised land" mentioned in 1 Nephi 20:23 was "believed to be on the coast of Chili, S. America," and he celebrated the Church's new home in the Great Basin by noting that the "pastures...in all high places" found in 1 Nephi 21:10 were, in fact, "the elevated regions of the Rocky Mountains."[19] Never before had a *Book of Mormon* edition included such formal linkages between the text's narrative and sites on the contemporary globe. Pratt used such geographic references to serve a double purpose: to indicate where events in the book actually took place and to underline the veracity of the book by invoking real places known to the contemporary reader.

Even with Pratt's careful work on the *Book of Mormon*'s text and its apparatus, his greatest contribution to the evolution of the book was his choice

Orson Pratt is pictured here around the time he began his
work on producing a new edition of the *Book of Mormon*.
A missionary, scientist, and theologian, Pratt was one of
the first great scholars of the book. Courtesy of the Church
Archives, The Church of Jesus Christ of Latter-day Saints

to abandon the chapter and paragraph markings of
previous editions. He replaced the book's old format with a new system of shorter chapter and verse
indicators that echoed the Bible editions of the day.
In fact, while earlier editions of the *Book of Mormon* read much more like a novel or historical work,
the 1879 edition took on the air of a sacred, biblical

text. Readers familiar with the Bible would see just how closely the *Book of Mormon* had come to reproducing a similar reading experience through Pratt's changes in textual presentation.

This move toward formatting the *Book of Mormon* like the Bible reached its fullest manifestation in James E. Talmage's 1920 revised edition of the book. The 1920 edition discontinued the use of Pratt's numerous geographical footnotes, but it did present the text in two columns and added dates to each page. This new chronological device helped readers grasp that the Lord had commanded Nephi to build a ship to cross to the Americas around 592 BCE, and that Samuel the righteous Lamanite prophesied Jesus's death and resurrection roughly five years before the birth of Christ.[20] Since 1920, all LDS editions of the *Book of Mormon* have appeared in a double-column format with an accompanying chronology, both common formatting practices found in American Bibles since the time of the American Revolution.[21]

The biblical formatting strategies of both Pratt and Talmage underline the eighth Mormon Article of Faith: "We believe the Bible to be the word of God as far as it is translated correctly; we also believe the Book of Mormon to be the word of God." The Utah Saints, however, had shown several signs by 1879 that they paid less attention to the *Book of Mormon* than they did to the Bible.[22] The book had

Different formats of the same page from two editions of the *Book of Mormon*. By 1920, editors had placed the text in two columns, and they had added short chapter summaries, verse markings, footnotes, and even a time-line marker in the bottom corner. 1830: courtesy Lilly Library, Indiana University, Bloomington, IN; 1920

been pivotal in founding the religious tradition, but by the late nineteenth century it still had not gained a place as a central text to guide Mormon theology. Grant Underwood, a scholar of nineteenth-century Mormonism, has convincingly argued that the Church's early leaders were far more likely to use the Bible in their sermons and teaching than they were the *Book of Mormon*. He writes that "compared to the Bible, the Book of Mormon was hardly cited at all."[23] Even in the Nauvoo period when Joseph was still with the Saints, the Bible was twenty times more likely to be cited in Mormon literature and sermons than was the *Book of Mormon*.[24]

The reasons for such a marked preference for the Bible over the *Book of Mormon* in the nineteenth century are complex, but they can, in part, be tied to the fact that the Bible was a well-established and widely revered sacred text. Those who taught from it were instantly credentialed by centuries of biblically centered Christian tradition.[25] Listeners, especially in the Bible-saturated print culture of the nineteenth century, would likely be more familiar with the Bible's contents and more conditioned to accept its divinely inspired status than they would be with a newer sacred text such as the *Book of Mormon*.

The *Book of Mormon* may have also been cited less among early Mormon leaders because of how it was overshadowed in many ways by the importance and uniqueness of many of Joseph's later revelations. These later revelations involved teachings on polygamy, baptism for the dead, and the plurality of gods. Although it can be argued that some of these doctrines are touched upon in the *Book of Mormon*, the most explicit teachings on these beliefs are not found in the book.[26] As a result, Mormons turned to revelations outside the *Book of Mormon* to help explain the distinctive nature of their tradition's identity and to help guide their religious practice.

As the twentieth century dawned, the book continued to be less emphasized in many of the Church's teaching settings. One reason for this lack of emphasis can be traced back to the fact that many leading Mormon scholars of the period had turned to non-Mormon institutions such as the University of Chicago to pursue advanced religion degrees.[27] When such scholars returned to teach at places like Brigham Young University (BYU) or in the Church Educational System (CES), they often brought with them approaches to the *Book of Mormon* that echoed the modernist tendencies in the German Higher Criticism so favored in many segments of liberal American Protestant and academic biblical study. Such study had come to see "the Bible as a collection of myths and folklore."[28] A number of influential BYU faculty members represented a growing tendency among Mormon intellectuals to see the book as mere allegory, not historical fact. Inevitably, such thinking among influential teachers at BYU and in the CES reverberated throughout the Church.

One can even detect in this period a de-emphasis on the *Book of Mormon* in certain missionary endeavors, activities where the book had stood as an unrivaled evangelistic tool since the Church's founding. The Saints had long pointed to the book as a distinctive guide for their brand of Christianity and as a vivid sign that God still wished to be intimately involved with his creation. Such an emphasis receded in certain mission efforts in the opening decades of the twentieth century when Ben E. Rich, the president of the Southern States and Eastern States Missions, developed a program that emphasized the Bible over the *Book of Mormon* in early discussions with potential converts.[29] Especially in the country's southern states, where the Bible was particularly well known among American Protestants, the reasoning for such an emphasis may well have centered on a strategy of engaging non-Mormons with a sacred text they knew before moving on to a sacred text they did not. Rich's method hinged on using the Bible to argue against standard Protestant views of suspended inspiration and a closed canon.[30] In this manner, a discussion of a well-accepted book like the Bible paved the way for investigations into the less well-known *Book of Mormon*. Rich's emphasis on the Bible over the *Book of Mormon* in initial conversations with converts would appear in missionary training guides until the 1960s.

To counteract the rising skepticism of the book's historicity and its receding role in missions, various countermovements arose within the LDS Church. By the 1930s, Church leaders had begun taking steps to safeguard the doctrinal teaching found at BYU and in other Church-sponsored educational settings by making sure all teachers adhered to the Church leadership's views on the absolute historical veracity and inspired nature of the book. Over time, teachers who viewed the *Book of Mormon* as nothing but a mythic tale were forced to find work elsewhere. As Church leaders monitored the doctrinal integrity of the Church's teachers and intellectuals, there arose a movement within the Church to prove the historicity of the book through the use of archaeological evidence.

One of the most important figures in this archaeological movement was Thomas Ferguson, a University of California–trained lawyer who developed a lifelong passion for Mesoamerican history and culture. Ferguson's devotion to connecting the *Book of Mormon* to actual historical events and geographic locations led him in 1951 to approach Church leaders with a formal plan to mount archaeological expeditions in the Tehuantepec area (the place earlier Mormon scholars had identified as the *Book of Mormon*'s "narrow neck of land" mentioned in the Book of Alma).[31] He was utterly convinced that these expeditions would bring forth artifacts that would "speak eloquently from the dust" to support the *Book of Mormon*.[32] The Church did not see this as the moment to provide financial support for such endeavors, but Ferguson pushed ahead and raised his own funding for the expedition. In 1952, he established the New World Archaeological Foundation (NWAF), an organization designed largely to facilitate the study of the book's connection to Mesoamerican ruins. For several years, he served as the foundation's president. Eventually his persistence and passion paid off, and by 1953 the Church began financially supporting certain aspects of the NWAF's work with sizable monetary gifts.[33]

As the work of the NWAF matured in the early 1960s, Ferguson remained utterly convinced that its expeditions would find Nephite and Lamanite cities, as well as other sites, proving the *Book of Mormon*'s historical veracity. Ferguson was to be sorely disappointed. Although the NWAF completed valuable archaeological work in southern Mexico and the surrounding regions, it did not uncover a single archaeological site or inscription that could be conclusively matched to the *Book of Mormon*'s narrative. In a letter to a friend just a few years before his death, Ferguson wrote, "[Y]ou can't set the Book-of-Mormon geography down anywhere—because it is fictional and will never meet the requirements of the dirt-archeology. I should say—what is in the ground will never conform to what is in the book."[34] By the mid-1970s, Ferguson had concluded that while the *Book of Mormon* was a mythic tale of great religious value, it had no basis in actual human history. As a result, his faith faltered, and he became what one scholar has described as "a closet doubter," a man who remained in the Church, but without any belief in the historical character of the *Book of Mormon* or Joseph's ability to translate ancient writings.[35]

Various attacks on the *Book of Mormon* via the German Higher Criticism, a lack of archaeological evidence, and a reluctance among many Saints to use the book as the fundamental element in Church evangelism met their most formidable foe in the towering intellectual figure of Hugh Nibley (1910–2005). Incredibly erudite and able to conduct research in more than a dozen languages, Nibley became a professor of history and religion at BYU in 1946.[36] He wrote extensively on the Church's sacred scriptures, and perhaps his greatest contribution to Mormon scripture research was his basic scholarly approach. As opposed to Ferguson's concentration on validating the book through Mesoamerican archaeology, Nibley emphasized the *Book of Mormon*'s rootedness in the various cultures of the ancient Middle East.

Nibley devoted himself to examining the *Book of Mormon* by using the widest possible Middle Eastern cultural lens. He set forth the "innumerable small coincidences" and cultural traces that confirmed the book's truth by showing its thorough

Hugh Nibley, pictured here at work in 1969, is widely regarded in LDS circles as one of the twentieth century's greatest academic scholars of Mormon sacred texts. Courtesy L. Tom Perry Special Collections, Harold B. Lee Library, Brigham Young University

"Egypticity" and "Arabicity."[37] Nibley argued that a close examination of the *Book of Mormon*'s multifaceted nature using the lenses of Middle Eastern linguistics, religion, politics, geography, and history would reveal it to be an ancient sacred text no less authentic than the Bible itself.[38] Nibley believed that only through a broad and capacious study of the book in the context of ancient Middle Eastern culture could one prove the text's authenticity.

Nibley pursued an analysis of the book that immersed it in the Middle East, not in the Americas.[39] In so doing, he effectively sidestepped the fact that not a single artifact or inscription had been located in the Americas to confirm the *Book of Mormon* as an actual historical document.[40] The highly academic nature and sheer volume of his research influenced a wide range of Mormons during his distinguished career, including a group of scholars who uncovered an altar in Yemen that might stand as the first hard archaeological evidence validating the *Book of Mormon*'s contents. Certain letters on this altar possibly correspond to the place name "Nahom" referred to by Nephi as his party passed through this Middle Eastern region.[41]

Nibley's research in general, and his Middle Eastern approach in particular, invigorated intellectual LDS approaches to the *Book of Mormon* throughout the latter half of the twentieth century. The gravitas of his scholarship aided Church leaders as they moved in 1961 to make the study of the *Book of Mormon* the required religion course for all BYU freshmen, as well as to increase the book's presence throughout the CES curricula beginning around the same time.[42] Nibley's influence on increasing the importance of the *Book of Mormon* within Mormonism is also seen in his presence at a meeting with the Church's top leadership in the

Salt Lake Temple in the late 1960s, when it was revealed that the *Book of Mormon* was not being emphasized enough in the Church's mission work.[43] Church leaders were immensely aided by the academic underpinnings that Nibley's work offered as they worked to change this emphasis. Emblematic of the Church's new desire to place the *Book of Mormon* in the foreground of their missions and teaching efforts, revised Church manuals began in 1973 to instruct the Saints to introduce the book in their initial discussion with any potential convert.[44] As a result, through ever-widening concentric circles emanating from the Church's educational and missionary efforts, the *Book of Mormon* came to enjoy an ever-larger place in the hearts and minds of Church members as the twentieth century progressed.

Even with the growing presence of the *Book of Mormon* within the Church after World War II, the fact remained that in many important Church settings the book continued to lack visibility. Between 1942 and 1986, the highest leaders of the Church cited the *Book of Mormon* a mere 12 percent of the time when they sought to support their comments with scripture in General Conference addresses.[45] This failure to recognize the book in such addresses changed radically when Ezra Taft Benson (1899–1994) became the Church's president in 1985. Benson used his 1986 General Conference address to inaugurate a presidency marked by a "vision of flooding the earth with the Book of Mormon."[46]

Throughout his life, Benson venerated the *Book of Mormon*, reading it daily for guidance on both large and small decisions.[47] He was utterly convinced of the book's centrality to the Church's spiritual life and passionately believed that in "this age of the electronic media and the mass distribution of the printed word, God will hold us accountable if we do not now move the Book of Mormon in a monumental way."[48] From the moment he assumed the prophet's mantle, Benson constantly affirmed the importance of the book, encouraging Mormons to study it daily because it could bring "a person nearer to God...than any other book."[49] He wished all Saints to recommit themselves to reading the book and spreading its message, so that the Church might not face "God's condemnation for having treated it lightly."[50] Benson carried his emphasis on the book to all the educational institutions of the Church, where again and again he sought to place the *Book of Mormon* at "the center of all gospel study."[51] He encouraged scholars at BYU not only to teach the book with renewed energy, but to study it with ever greater scholarly care.

After decades of increasing scholarly interest and institutional emphasis on the book, Benson is per-

Ezra Taft Benson wished his presidency to be marked by a "vision of flooding the earth with the Book of Mormon." Courtesy of the Church Archives, The Church of Jesus Christ of Latter-day Saints

haps most accurately described as a kind of culminating catalyst whose presidency served as a tipping point within the Church that propelled the *Book of Mormon* to the forefront of LDS consciousness. His clarion call for believers to engage with the *Book of Mormon* was carried on by succeeding presidents of the Church. In 2005, then LDS Church president Gordon Hinckley challenged every member to "read or reread the Book of Mormon."[52] Thus since the 1980s the LDS Church has engaged its founding text with unprecedented energy and resources.

The LDS Church's commitment to the *Book of Mormon* at the turn of the twenty-first century differed significantly from that of the next largest body of Mormons, the RLDS (or newly renamed Community of Christ). While the LDS Church had a history of ignoring the *Book of Mormon* during its first century, the Community of Christ had paid greater attention to the book in its formative years. These roles were clearly reversed by the year 2000, as the leaders of the two Mormon churches took radically different positions on the text. Those at the highest levels of the Community of Christ questioned the book's value and its historicity, while LDS leaders changed the subtitle of the book in 1982 in their printed editions to read, *Another Testament of Jesus Christ*. LDS Church leaders wished to make it unmistakably clear that the *Book of Mormon* was every bit as inspired and important as the Bible itself.[53]

Benson's presidency ushered in a new era for the *Book of Mormon* among Latter-day Saints. In the closing decades of the twentieth century, the extreme seriousness with which the book was treated brought forth a flowering of translation, intellectual, and artistic work connected to the text. To an unprecedented degree, the *Book of Mormon* was taking center stage in the life of the LDS Church.

Flowering

PART III

Therefore, go forth unto this people,

and declare the words which I have spoken,

unto the ends of the earth.

—3 Nephi 11:41

Missionary Work and the Book

CHAPTER 5

While the *Book of Mormon* has occupied different rungs of importance over the years on the ladder of the LDS Church's religious educational programming, there is one area of practice where, setting aside a brief period of de-emphasis in the early twentieth century, it has long retained preeminence: missions work. The three witnesses to the golden plates expressed the desire that the book's truth might be "known unto all nations, kindred, tongues, and people," a desire that set a tone of missionary zeal that has never wavered among the Saints.[1] By the beginning of the twenty-first century, more than fifty thousand such missionaries were serving the Church in over 160 countries.[2] Even those who know little of Mormonism are often familiar with the pairs of conservatively dressed men and modestly clad women who travel door-to-door sharing their Gospel message.

The Church's missionary fervor began immediately after its founding in April 1830. Joseph instituted an aggressive program of proselytization just weeks after E. B. Grandin produced the first copies of the *Book of Mormon*. As soon as new converts were baptized, he commissioned the able-bodied men among them to go forth and spread the new Mormon Gospel. In the Church's earliest days, most missionary commissions lasted only a few weeks and were modeled on the evangelistic travels of Jesus's own disciples, who moved from town to town without supplies or money, totally dependent on God's provision and guidance. Such journeys were extreme exercises in faith, but exercises that exposed a growing number of Americans to a new Gospel message.

While these early missionaries spoke to everyone they met during their travels, it quickly became apparent that their greatest successes came among people with whom they had some prior relationship. Throughout the 1830s and 1840s, Mormonism spread most readily through family and already-established social connections.[3] The pronounced linkage between such relational ties and conversion rates still prevails today as people who are connected socially or through family ties to Church members are ten times more likely to become Mormons than those simply contacted by the Church's missionaries.[4]

Throughout the nineteenth century, the *Book of Mormon* stood as the most central testimony in all evangelistic activity. Missionaries and members might speak of the work of the Holy Spirit, the communal vision of the Saints, or the restored apostolic authority of the Church, but in the end, it was because of the *Book of Mormon* that the Church existed. The Saints eagerly pointed to the book as the most tangible proof that God had restored his true Church to the earth. One convert in Onondaga County, New York, captured the effect of the missionary's message when he wrote that the "golden Bible . . . struck me like a shock of electricity."[5] It was the book that stood as the single greatest testimony that God was indeed doing something new in the world.

Aside from how it testified to a new prophetic religious tradition, the *Book of Mormon* also served as a missionary guide. From the Church's earliest days, the book helped determine the direction for its missionary activity. Just months after organizing his Church, Joseph sent missionaries to the Catteraugus tribe near Buffalo, New York, a group he believed to be ancestors of the Lamanites. Although their visit lasted but a day, the missionaries did leave two copies of the *Book of Mormon* for members of the tribe who could read.[6]

In the first two decades of the Church's existence, missionaries not only spread throughout New England and the country's western frontier, but they also traveled first to Canada and then in 1837 across the Atlantic to Great Britain. So successful was the Church's England mission that throughout much of the nineteenth century conversion rates in that country exceeded those in America.[7] By the 1850s, Mormon leaders were strategizing about how best to enable the thirty thousand Latter-day Saints located in England to emigrate and gather in God's new Zion of Utah.[8]

The success of the English mission encouraged the Church's leadership to look elsewhere to spread their message. Because of the critical place of the *Book of Mormon* in early missionary work, a broader mission field inevitably led to the first translations of the book into different languages. The first such language was Danish. Strangely enough, it was a translation that began not on foreign shores, but in Nauvoo, Illinois, where Peter Olsen Hansen, a convert with Danish roots, began translating the book into his native tongue.[9] In 1849, Hansen was called along with Erastus Snow to serve as missionaries in Scandinavia. Snow, a member of the Quorum of the Twelve Apostles and a man who had a deep appreciation for the power of printed material in evangelistic efforts, encouraged Hansen to complete his translation quickly. A mere twelve months after their arrival in Copenhagen, a finished edition of a Danish *Book of Mormon* appeared in May 1851.[10]

Although Hansen's Danish translation was the first foreign-language edition of the *Book of Mormon*, others followed almost immediately. In the next year, four new translations appeared: German, French, Italian, and Welsh.[11] These editions were printed locally in most cases in such cities as Hamburg, Paris, and Georgetown (Wales). Only with the centralization of the Church's printing operations in the 1870s did Salt Lake City begin to play a major role in publishing foreign-language editions of the *Book of Mormon*.[12]

Of particular interest in the early foreign mission work of the Church were its activities in Hawaii and other South Sea island networks. Over time, LDS Church leaders undergirded the Church's extensive missionary work in these islands by stating that these isolated spots were, in fact, populated by Lamanites, descendants of Lehi, who had left the Americas around 50 BCE to sail into unknown regions of the Pacific Ocean.[13] Missionary work to these islands dates all the way back to Joseph, who commissioned Addison Pratt, a former whaler who had learned Hawaiian during his travels, to be the Church's first missionary to preach the Mormon Gospel in a language other than English.[14]

Addison (no relation to the famous Parley and Orson Pratt) became one of the most successful missionaries of his generation, as he preached in Hawaii and French Polynesia on various tours from 1844 to 1852. His work was so successful that by 1848 more than eighteen thousand South Sea islanders had converted to Mormonism.[15] His evangelistic efforts paved the way for the translation of the *Book of Mormon* into Hawaiian (1855) and the establishment of a particularly strong Church presence in a variety of Pacific islands beyond Hawaii, including Tahiti, Bora Bora, and Tubuai.[16] Eventually Mormon missionary work extended throughout the South Pacific and enjoyed considerable success in Fiji and Samoa, and among the Maori people of New Zealand. As a result of this particularly strong Mormon missionary presence in the Pacific, many island populations were early recipients of their own translations of the *Book of Mormon*.[17]

During the ensuing century, the number of foreign-language editions of the *Book of Mormon* increased at a slow, steady rate. By 1970, the *Book of Mormon*, as a whole or in part, was available in twenty-three languages. The 1970s saw a radical increase in the appearance of new language translations under the leadership of President Spencer Kimball (1895–1985), owing in large measure to the rapid globalization of the Church's mission work during these years. Between 1972 and 1979, the Church published eleven new translations of the book, an almost 30 percent increase in production over the first 140 years. The rapid rise in translations was made possible to a great extent by the Church's decision to translate only portions of the book in a given language as a stepping-stone to a later translation of the entire book. When such selections were offered, they shied away from the book's historical content and concentrated instead on important doctrinal matters, particularly prophecies and testimony of Jesus Christ.[18]

Another great emphasis during the 1970s translation period was centered on Native American populations. President Kimball felt a particular burden to preach the Mormon Gospel to the "some 60,000,000 Indians or Lamanites who carry the precious blood of Lehi in their veins."[19] Kimball lamented that the Lord had "not forgotten the Lamanites, but sometimes I think we may have."[20] With these native populations in mind, Kimball spurred on translation work to various native populations in North, Central, and South America, including the Kekchi, Navajo, and Mayan.

When Ezra Taft Benson ascended to the Church presidency upon Kimball's death in 1985, he continued his predecessor's extensive *Book of Mormon* translation program as part of his unwavering commitment to foregrounding the book's importance throughout the Church. Thus the 1980s became a pivotal decade for the book in terms of foreign-language editions. An astounding forty-nine new language editions or partial editions appeared in the 1980s, eleven in the 1990s, and nearly twenty in the first decade of the twenty-first century.[21] Of particular interest within this remarkable growth was the translation work done in Eastern Europe and in Africa. After the fall of the Berlin Wall in 1989, Mormon missionaries spread throughout Eastern Europe, following a long-established Church policy that LDS missionaries enter only those countries where national governments have given their approval for such religious activity. As countries opened their doors to the West, Mormon missionaries ventured into places they had never before gone. Such missionary work led to the translation of the *Book of Mormon* into several new Eastern European languages, including Ukrainian, Albanian, Estonian, Lithuanian, Slovenian, and Serbian.

As missionary work expanded in Eastern Europe, similar strides were being made in Africa. The opening of Africa as a vibrant Church mission field was due in large part to the Church's reversal in 1978 of its long-standing policy denying its priesthood to any male who had black African ancestry.[22] Although the issue of African Americans and the priesthood is a bit murky in the earliest days of Mormonism, by the 1850s Brigham Young was codifying the doctrine that those of African descent could not hold the priesthood.[23] To differing degrees, both Joseph and Young shared a racial view popular in their day based on the belief that Africans were descended from Noah's cursed son, Ham.[24] The curse of Ham, a stain often traced back to Adam's murderous son Cain, was frequently invoked in antebellum religious thought to explain the degraded condition and character of those of African descent. Young was particularly vocal in popularizing such views among the Saints, and by 1852 he was teaching that "[a]ny man having one drop of the seed of Cane [Cain] in him cannot hold the priesthood," and "if any man mingles his seed with the seed of Cane the only way he could get rid of it or have salvation would be to come forward & have his head cut off & spill his blood upon the ground."[25]

Joseph and Young may have been products of their historical moment in terms of their views on race, but the *Book of Mormon* itself reinforced their racial positions. In 2 Nephi the book states that those who have hardened their hearts against God experienced a "sore cursing" as the "Lord God did cause a skin of blackness to come upon them."[26] Later, in the Book of Alma, we are told that "the skins of the Lamanites were dark, according to the mark which was set upon their fathers, which was a curse upon them because of their transgression and their rebellion."[27] Such statements continued to inform the attitude of Church leaders on the cursed nature of dark skin well into the twentieth century. Apostle Bruce R. McConkie (1915–1985), one of the Church's most influential thinkers of the mid-twentieth century, wrote in his widely read—although not officially Church-sanctioned—*Mormon Doctrine* that "the gospel message of salvation is not carried affirmatively" to blacks, and that "Negroes in this life are denied the priesthood; under no circumstances can they hold this delegation of authority from the Almighty."[28] Owing to this belief in the cursed nature of those with dark skins, the Church expended little missionary effort toward Africans for nearly a century and a half.

Beliefs centered on the degraded state of those of African descent changed radically on June 8, 1978, when Church president Spencer W. Kimball announced a new revelation. He declared that "all worthy male members of the Church may be ordained to the priesthood without regard for race or color."[29] Black males were no longer outside the fold. They could enjoy every privilege accorded to other races and ethnic groups within the Church. Kimball's revelation energized the Church's missionary work in Africa, and translation work on the *Book of Mormon* reflected this new engagement with the African continent.

Prior to 1983, the *Book of Mormon* had not been translated into a single native African language, although it was available in such languages as English and Portuguese, making it accessible to certain literate populations in African nations including Liberia, Tanzania, South Africa, Zimbabwe, Mozambique, and Angola. Translations in French and German also allowed Africans in Côte d'Ivoire, the Congo, and Cameroon to read the book. In 1983, the Church published selections of the *Book of Mormon* in Efik and Kisii, making the book accessible for the first time in the native tribal languages of Nigeria and Kenya. Beginning in 2000, the Church turned a great deal of its translation energy to rendering the entire book into native African tongues such as Ibo (Nigeria), Xhosa (South Africa), Swahili (Congo, Uganda, Somalia, and Tanzania), Tswana (Botswana), Fante (Ghana), and Zulu (South Africa and Zimbabwe). Since 1983, the *Book of Mormon* has appeared in twelve native African languages.

The radical increase in *Book of Mormon* translation work over the past half century has forced the Church both to systematize its method for picking language targets for new translations and also to establish a common set of standards ensuring that new editions of the *Book of Mormon* remain true to the spirit and content of the Church's most current recognized edition of the book. Aside from imperatives sent down by the Church's prophet, such as Kimball's emphasis on Native American populations, the Church's leadership has developed in the past five decades a clear selection rubric when it comes to choosing new languages for *Book of Mormon* translation work. In the main, the rubric has a grassroots emphasis. It pays close attention to the number of a language group's baptized Church members and its number of organized congregations. It also takes into account the number of speakers of the language more generally and the perceived receptivity of those speakers to the Mormon Gospel.[30]

Once it has become clear that a given language group has a pronounced need for materials in their own language, the Church strives to make these materials available. In its attempt to establish religious terms and ideas, the first materials the Church offers are missionary in nature, followed by educational texts on doctrine and practice. Only after such works have been circulated does the Church turn its attention to providing a translation of the *Book of Mormon*. The Church does not include Bible translation in its missionary vision. Viable

Bible translations produced by other translating bodies, such as national and international Bible societies, are quickly adopted by the Church. The Church focuses its efforts entirely on producing its own unique scriptures in new languages.

After the Church leadership has commissioned a *Book of Mormon* in a new language, it works hard to identify one or two native translators to train to do the arduous and challenging work of scriptural translation. The translation tasks are done almost entirely in the countries in which the newly translated *Book of Mormon* will be used. The major exception to this local preference is Spanish. Over the years, the Church has adopted a type of global Spanish version of the *Book of Mormon* to use in the numerous countries in which Spanish is spoken, although different countries can have significantly different dialects of Spanish, inflected by centuries of development in different geographical locations. Thus Spanish speakers in countries such as Spain, Argentina, and Mexico all have the same translation of the *Book of Mormon*. The translation and oversight for this global Spanish version is centered in the Church headquarters in Salt Lake City. Locating this Spanish translation work in Utah has allowed the Church to enjoy great efficiency in producing the Spanish *Book of Mormon*, as well as the added benefit of having the book originate from the

Church's headquarters, granting it a special authority, and thus acceptance, among the world's different Spanish-speaking populations.

This exception aside, almost all other translations
are worked on in the field. Once a native translator
is chosen (and such a translator has to be a member of the Church in good standing), the Church
then moves to train the person in translation work.
The translation manual as it currently stands includes some seven hundred pages of instructions,
examples, and drills to help translators achieve an
accurate version of the *Book of Mormon*. Of para-
mount importance for Church leaders is that any
new translation of the *Book of Mormon* attempt to
render as closely as possible the currently Church-
authorized English edition of the text.

In translation terminology, the Church is firmly
committed to formal equivalency. Formally equivalent translations seek to produce a word-for-word
translation of a given work. The Church embraces
formal equivalency because it believes that its
English-language version of the book is a product
of divine revelation. The English words were given
directly to Joseph to be set down and published.
Later editions of the book—the update comprising
some three thousand word changes in the 1837 edition being the most dramatic example—were also
accepted by the Church as divinely inspired. When

translating the English words of the currently authorized version into other languages, the Church attempts to render the words, not just the ideas these words convey, as accurately as possible.

The Church wishes each of its *Book of Mormon* translations to retain as much as possible the sentence structure, phrasing, and idioms of the original language. The alternative is called functional—or dynamic—equivalency in translation. Functional equivalency stresses a thought-for-thought process of translation bent on capturing the original text's meaning. Formal equivalency seeks to bring the reader back to the world of the ancient text, while functional equivalency seeks to transport that ancient text into the world of the modern reader.[31] The primary reason that the Church has no interest in a modern-language version of the *Book of Mormon* is that it would be, by necessity, a functional equivalency translation. The Church leadership believes that too much of the text's meaning, rooted in its inspired word selection, would be lost in an attempt to make its language modern.

In fact, the First Presidency of the Church has set down clear guidelines for translating the *Book of Mormon* to "preserve the doctrine and meaning of the original authors."[32] Central commands found in these guidelines include the following:

Be as literal as possible.

Follow very closely, the words, phrases, and sentence structure, as well as the idiomatic expressions and literary style of the original authors.

Include redundant expressions and awkward sentence structure.

Preserve the literary idiosyncrasies and style of each author.[33]

As a consequence, the Church trains its translators to pay close attention to both the language *and* the structure of the *Book of Mormon*'s core text.

Sophisticated textual aids, made available to translators, code every word found in the *Book of Mormon* in a manner that allows a translator to render a term such as "record" the same way throughout the text, depending on that word's varied part of speech and usage. Consistency throughout the text is as revered a translation goal as accuracy. "Plates of gold" is translated in such a way that it does not become "golden plates" or "plates made of gold." Every instance of the much-repeated phrase "and it came to pass" is faithfully included, as are sentence fragments and other cases of nonstandard grammar. Translators are to be true to the English text given them; they are to avoid correcting it or interpreting it as they do their work.

In a similar manner, translators are instructed to maintain as much as possible the archaic English forms of the words contained in the book, as well as the sentence structure itself. For example, translators are taught to pay close attention to the chiasmic sentence structures found throughout the *Book of Mormon*. A chiasm (referring to the cross shape of the Greek letter chi, χ) is a structure that works on the principles of inversion, reflection, and focus. A passage from 1 Nephi 1:2–3 provides an example of chiasm used to train translators:

A. Having had a great **knowledge** of the goodness . . .
B.   I **make** a record of my proceedings . . .
C.   yea I **make**
D.   a **record**
E.   in the **language** of my father
F.   Which consists of the **learning** . . .
E.   And the **language** of the Eyptians
D.   And I know that the **record**
C   Which I **make** is true
B.   And I **make** it with my own hand
A. I make it according to my **knowledge**

Through such a structure, sentences focus on particular themes and meanings. In this case from First Nephi, learning is the central thought, supported by notes on the importance of language, records, writing, and knowledge. Translators are drilled to retain as much as possible of this structure and the meaning it underlines.

Once a translator has finished a substantial section of his or her work, the translation is reviewed by one or two other translators, who check the work for accuracy and consistency. After this review process is completed, and differences of opinion are adjudicated and settled, a larger group of native language speakers then review the material. Supervisors from the Church's Translation Department in Salt Lake City enter the process at several points to make sure the work is proceeding according to the standards and goals of the Church. Finally, the translation supervisors will make a recommendation to the Church's leadership to accept the new translation of the *Book of Mormon*.

In the normal course of events, a new translation of the *Book of Mormon,* from the point it is initiated as a translation project to its final approval, takes on average 4.8 years. Some language translations have been completed much more quickly. The Latvian edition took only eighteen months to complete and then another six months to go through the publishing process. Other languages have taken much longer.

The Urdu translation of the *Book of Mormon* took fifteen years to complete. It is a particularly instructive case, illuminating the various challenges of translation work. The actual Urdu translation work took five years to finish, but once the book entered the production process, problems arose. These problems centered on obtaining a font deemed appropriate for the book's printing. In order to meet the target audience's expectations for a sacred text, a particular Nastaliq Arabic script style was the only option. Unfortunately, no computer font existed that could represent this style, so the Church's graphic designers set about hand-drawing a font set that captured the stylized Arabic-based script. These artists had to compose what amounted to a twenty thousand character set. The font creation process alone took some seven years of work. As a result, a translation that had begun in 1995 was not released to the public until 2007.[34]

Other formatting issues also underline the challenges of translation work. In certain Middle Eastern cultures, any printed page containing sacred writing frames the printed text with borders, highlighting the special status of the page's words. Thus the Church is careful to use page borders when printing its Persian (Farsi) edition of the *Book of Mormon*. In Japanese culture, white is the color of death; it is deemed highly inappropriate to print sacred words on such a color. As a consequence, the Church makes a point to print every copy of the Japanese *Book of Mormon* on cream-colored paper.

The challenges of bringing the book to the world reach well beyond translation strategies and type-setting conventions. The Church has gone to great lengths to determine exactly what materials should be used in the *Book of Mormon*'s production. No-where is this more apparent than in its production of even the most inexpensive missionary editions. Even though the Church will ultimately give away thousands of copies of these editions, it maintains a practice of using exceptionally high quality paper (currently imported from France) that will stand the test of time. This paper is extremely thin, offer-ing extra benefits such as a thinner volume that is less intimidating to potential readers, and a lighter weight, reducing distribution costs.

Along with the high quality of paper, the Church is committed to binding these missionary editions in the sturdiest manner possible. Knowing that mis-sionary editions will need to face all manner of cli-mates and conditions, the Church has moved away from using common animal-based glues in its bind-ing processes. It was observed that missionary edi-tions often disintegrated in hot and humid climates where such glues had a tendency to break down. As a result, the Church turned to a specially for-mulated polyurethane glue that remained intact in conditions of both extreme heat and extreme cold. To assess the binding's strength, the Church tested samples by heating them in high-powered drying machines, soaking and tumbling them in washing machines, and freezing them in refrigeration units. The Church wanted to be certain that a book containing eternal truths was being bound for eternity as well.

As concerned as the Church is with the quality of translating, printing, and binding the *Book of Mormon*, it pays an equal amount of attention to how the book is disseminated by its missionaries around the world. Each Mormon male in good standing between the ages of eighteen and twenty-six is expected to serve a two-year mission. Women may also go on missions, but their tenure is eighteen months in the field, although they are allowed to do their missions after the age of twenty-six. Currently the Church has approximately fifty-two thousand missionaries spreading the Mormon Gospel around the world. To equip this vast number of missionaries, the Church has fifteen internationally located Missionary Training Centers. The largest of these, in Provo, Utah, is a college-like campus with the capacity to train up to thirty-five hundred missionaries at a time.

The *Book of Mormon* has been translated into more than one hundred different languages, and the polyglot nature of the book is reflected in the curriculum offered in Provo's Training Center.

This center trains missionaries in more than fifty languages. The length of time missionaries spend at the center is directly tied to the language they will be using in their mission work. Those who are going on English-speaking missions spend nineteen days at the center; those who will be ministering in Romance languages spend nine weeks in training; while those learning non-Romance languages such as Chinese and Japanese spend the longest period at the center, eleven weeks. Almost all of the language training is done by eight hundred part-time instructors, most of whom are students at the neighboring Brigham Young University campus who have just returned from their own mission work.

While at the center, missionaries use as one of their key training textbooks *Preach My Gospel: A Guide to Missionary Service.* The *Guide* teaches Mormon missionaries to consider the *Book of Mormon* as their "main source for teaching restored truth," a principle that is reinforced by language instructors' use of the *Book of Mormon* as a central text in language-acquisition drills. As the *Guide* reminds every missionary, Joseph made the book's primacy clear: "Take away the Book of Mormon and the revelations, and where is our religion? We have none."[35] The distinctive character of Mormonism is firmly rooted in the *Book of Mormon,* as it stands as a testimony to God's restored priesthood and Church on the earth. To underline this message, the *Guide* invokes the words of Ezra Taft Benson, who pointed to the book as the single best response to anyone who objects to the teachings of Mormonism. Benson put it simply: "The only problem the objector has to resolve for himself is whether the Book of Mormon is true. For if the Book of Mormon is true, then Jesus is the Christ, Joseph Smith was his prophet, The Church of Jesus Christ of Latter-day Saints is true, and it is being led today by a prophet receiving revelation."[36] In this spirit, the *Guide* instructs missionaries to introduce the *Book of Mormon* as early as possible in their encounters with nonbelievers.[37]

The missionary emphasis on the *Book of Mormon* leads, in turn, to the Church's encouraging every missionary to read the book alongside anyone interested in Mormonism. The book contains incredibly complex narratives and themes, and such a shared reading experience enables the missionary to serve as a personal interpreter of many of the book's harder concepts and intricate plot lines. In the end, however, missionaries are taught to present the book to nonbelievers and have them ask God whether its contents are true. Invoking the words of Moroni, they encourage everyone who encounters the *Book of Mormon* to "ask God, the Eternal Father, in the name of Christ, if these things are not true; and if ye shall ask with a sincere heart, with real intent, having faith in Christ, he will manifest the truth of it unto you, by the power of the Holy Ghost."[38] Ultimately, confirmation of the book's truths is left to the workings of higher spiritual forces, not to the persuasive abilities of the missionary. All the while the message is clear: without the book there would be no Mormon religious tradition. If the book is false, so is every aspect of the Church built upon it.

Scholars and the Book

CHAPTER 6

Mormon missionaries are not the only people who desire readers of the *Book of Mormon* to take Moroni's words seriously by asking "God, the Eternal Father, in the name of Christ," whether the contents of the book are true.[1] Mormon children are encouraged at a young age to do the same, as are older Mormons whose faith may waver as they age. This emphasis on seeking divine confirmation to help guide one's religious convictions lies at the heart of Mormon belief and practice. Yet, while LDS Church leaders concentrate on a faith-based relationship with the text, the Church does have a long history of members who have valued a rationalist approach to the book as well.

Such members have sought to provide their fellow Saints with the highest levels of scholarly professionalism to reinforce the truth claims of the *Book of Mormon*. As the Church's emphasis on the book grew in the 1970s and 1980s, so did Mormon scholarly activity surrounding it. Hugh Nibley's work, described in chapter 4, is an integral part of this scholarship, but equally important was the formation of the Foundation for Ancient Research and Mormon Studies (FARMS) in 1979. By working together, Nibley and FARMS helped usher in a new era of scholarly engagement with the book.

John W. Welch, an attorney who first practiced law in Los Angeles and then joined the faculty of the law school at Brigham Young University (BYU) in 1980, originally established FARMS as a nonprofit collective that gathered and circulated scholarly pieces that elucidated various aspects of the contents and history of the *Book of Mormon* and other Mormon scriptures.[2] In 1984, FARMS began a partnership with Deseret Book Company to publish Nibley's collected works, thereby widening the readership for Nibley's writings within Church circles. Over the next sixteen years, FARMS published nineteen imposing volumes of Nibley's research.

While Nibley's scholarship provided the initial massive backbone to a larger FARMS public presence among Mormons, others soon joined forces with the foundation to produce highly influential works on the book. One of the most important of these scholars was John Sorenson, a longtime professor of anthropology at BYU, who published his highly influential *An Ancient American Setting for the Book of Mormon* (1985) through FARMS. In this volume and other later related works, Sorenson reinforced the cornerstone belief of the Church that "the Book of Mormon account actually did take place *some*where," by positing possible locations for the "real places where real Nephis and Almas did the things the volume says that they did."[3] Sorenson also became a key figure beginning in the 1980s for popularizing the view that while there still existed great uncertainty about the exact locations of various cities and events in the *Book of Mormon*, there were reasons enough for confidence that the book's primary events took place in the area surrounding the Isthmus of Tehuantepec in southern Mexico.[4]

It is important to note that Sorenson was not the first Mormon scholar to posit a Mesoamerican setting for the events depicted in the *Book of Mormon*. In the early 1840s, Joseph himself became attracted to a similar line of reasoning when he was introduced to John Lloyd Stephens's pathbreaking *Incidents of Travel in Central America, Chiapas and Yucatan* (1841). Stephens had just completed an extensive Central American expedition in the company of a gifted architectural artist by the name of Frederick Catherwood. His published account of his travels offered Americans the first extended English-language treatise on ancient Mayan

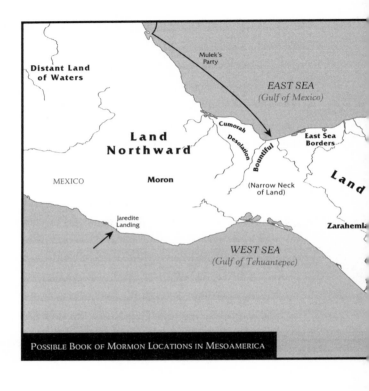

Distant Land
of Waters

Mulek's
Party

EAST SEA
(Gulf of Mexico)

Land
Northward

MEXICO

Cumorah

Desolation

Bountiful

East Sea
Borders

Moron

(Narrow Neck
of Land)

Land

Jaredite
Landing

WEST SEA
(Gulf of Tehuantepec)

Zarahemla

POSSIBLE BOOK OF MORMON LOCATIONS IN MESOAMERICA

civilization. Stephens's discussions of massive ancient cities, stone monuments, and hieroglyphic
writings—all of which were compellingly illustrated by Catherwood—helped convince Joseph
that the events in the *Book of Mormon* had taken
place in Central America.[5] He came to believe that
the ruins uncovered by Stephens and Catherwood
coincided with the *Book of Mormon*'s Land of Zara-

Possible locations for events found in the *Book of Mormon* based on the work of the anthropologist John Sorenson.

Map labels: MEXICO, BELIZE, GUATEMALA, HONDURAS, EL SALVADOR, Nephi, Lehi's Party, East or South Wilderness, Southward, N

hemla, and that the "small neck of land" separating various regions in the *Book of Mormon* was also located in southern Mexico.[6]

In the following decades, other Mormon scholars followed in Joseph's footsteps, tracing the connections between Mesoamerica and the book, but Sorenson would distinguish himself in this scholarly tradition by popularizing a limited-geography theory of the *Book of Mormon*. He posited that the civilizations recorded in the *Book of Mormon* inhabited an "area approximately 500 miles long and perhaps 200 miles wide" somewhere in Mesoamerica.[7] Sorenson drastically narrowed the geographical region of the *Book of Mormon*'s story by claiming that the book was a history not of two continents, but only of a small portion of one. He argued that the narrative should be considered the history of but one group of civilizations that occupied the ancient Americas, and in so doing he significantly reduced the possible range of criticism against the book. With this limited-geography line of argumentation, Sorenson provided a defense against those quick to debunk the belief that the book offers an accurate prehistory of the entire North American continent.

Sorenson's more restrictive theory of *Book of Mormon* geography was not entirely his own. Such thinking was already circulating to a significant degree within the Church. In 1981, the Church's leadership introduced a new prefatory section in their English-language editions of the *Book of Mormon* that reflected a less aggressive stance on the importance of the Nephites and the Lamanites to the Western Hemisphere's development. The book's new introduction described the Lamanites as "the principal ancestors of the American Indians," departing from the Church's previous, more expansive claim that every Native American was descended from Lamanite stock.[8] Thus Sorenson did not originate a more constricted view of *Book of Mormon* geography, but his extensive research did much to legitimize the limited-geography view of the book within the Church.

FARMS has continued to sponsor and publish profoundly influential scholarship among Church members on the *Book of Mormon*. Since 1985, it has produced thirty-three books focused exclusively on the *Book of Mormon*, and in 1992 it founded a scholarly periodical, the *Journal of Book of Mormon Studies* (renamed in 2008 the *Journal of Book of Mormon and Other Restoration Scripture*).[9] FARMS gained such stature within the Church that it became a formally recognized part of BYU in 1997, amplifying still further its scholarly voice within Church circles. In 2006, BYU incorporated FARMS into the Neal A. Maxwell Institute, an umbrella organization for some of the most scholarly Church-related research on ancient manuscripts that claim origins in the Americas and the Middle East.

FARMS has also played an important apologetic role within the Church when disputes concerning the book's historicity have arisen. Through its scholarship, FARMS has sought to answer the Church's many critics who have attacked the book's historical accuracy from any number of angles, including, but not limited to, the suspiciously large population sizes mentioned in the book; the claims that barley, horses, and steel existed in the Americas long before the dates suggested by all known archaeological evidence; and the host of linguistic questions that arise from plates supposedly written in "Reformed Egyptian."[10] FARMS has stood on the scholarly front line against such attacks, often providing elaborately reasoned answers to rebut negative views of the book.

At the turn of the twenty-first century, certain scientifically minded members of the Church turned to DNA research to help prove that there exists a genetic link between the Middle East and Native Americans.[11] Just as Thomas Ferguson and his New World Archaeological Foundation began to pursue archaeological research in the 1950s to prove the historical reliability of the *Book of Mormon*, more recent Mormon academics have turned their attention to genetics with a similar hope. Through analyzing DNA groupings found in both the Middle East and the Americas, they sought evidence that at least some portion of the Native American population descended from Middle Eastern ancestors.

A significant player in such research was BYU microbiologist Scott Woodward, who in 2000, with the help of philanthropists Ira Fulton and James

Sorenson, launched a multimillion-dollar study to gather genetic information to link past and present human beings.[12] Like the New World Archaeological Foundation before it, Woodword's Molecular Genealogy Research Group (MGRG) completed a great deal of valuable work, but produced little to defend the *Book of Mormon* as either an ancient or a historically accurate text. In the case of DNA research, the work of the MGRG offered no compelling counterevidence to debunk the reigning theory that Native Americans are descended from Asiatic gene pools, not Middle Eastern ones.[13] In the words of anthropologist Thomas Murphy, "While DNA shows that ultimately all human populations are closely related, to date no intimate genetic link has been found between ancient Israelites and indigenous Americans, much less within the time frame suggested by the Book of Mormon."[14] Throughout the quest for DNA confirmation of the antiquity and veracity of the *Book of Mormon*'s narrative, FARMS has kept abreast of and engaged in debates surrounding DNA research.[15]

As was the case in the 1950s and 1960s with the apologetics promise of archaeological evidence, the Church has flirted with DNA evidence as a way to prove the historical accuracy of the *Book of Mormon*. It has not taken a formal stand, however, on the issue. Science has upon occasion enticed

Church leaders with the promise of confirmation for the text's claims, but no scientific evidence has ever emerged to prove conclusively the historical truth of any event or location in the book. Thus Church leaders continue to emphasize that one's relationship to the *Book of Mormon* and the religious practice it engenders is based on personal revelatory confirmation and is primarily a matter of faith.

While FARMs was establishing itself as a central hub for advanced scholarship concerning the *Book of Mormon*, another scholar arose in the 1980s who brought a different kind of academic expertise to bear on the study of the book. During these years, Royal Skousen, a BYU professor of linguistics and English, began a monumental study attempting to reconstruct the most accurate version of the book's original 1830 text. Over the next twenty years, Skousen employed cutting-edge linguistic theories and bibliographic technologies to help establish the purest English urtext of the *Book of Mormon*. In his quest, Skousen employed such diverse means as computer-driven linguistic modeling, ultraviolet photography, and multispectral imaging to examine the words recorded in the oldest extant manuscripts and editions of the book to arrive at the exact text Joseph initially wished to present to the world.[16]

Skousen based his work on the "two manuscripts and twenty textually significant printed editions (ranging from 1830 to 1981)" of the book.[17] In his re-creation of Joseph's original text, Skousen sought to eliminate typesetting mistakes, scribal errors, and incorrect conjectural textual emendations. He then spent years determining the words Joseph most probably dictated to his scribes. Examples abound in Skousen's work where his "earliest text" differs from the current 1981 LDS standard edition, but one can get a taste for his project by looking at 1 Nephi 8:31. There the 1981 text reads "multitudes **feeling** their way," while Skousen argues that the original text read "multitudes **pressing** their way."[18] He attributes this particular change to Oliver Cowdery's misreading another scribe's handwriting while preparing the printer's manuscript for E. B. Grandin's typesetter. In 2009, Skousen published *The Book of Mormon: The Earliest Text*, a work many considered "the definitive scholarly version of the Book of Mormon."[19] Because this single work could not encompass his more than two decades of bibliographic scholarship, with the help of FARMS Skousen also published a six-volume set entitled *Analysis of Textual Variants of the Book of Mormon.*[20]

Because the *Book of Mormon* is a living text, open to revision by the Church's inspired leader and prophet at any time, Skousen's work is not expected to impel the Church's leadership to revise the currently authorized 1981 edition to any great extent.

The Church revises the book only as is necessitated by revelation, not in response to recovery work such as Skousen's. Joseph himself revised the book twice after its appearance in 1830, so while Skousen's work to establish the most accurate 1830 text may be of great interest to scholars, it is of less use to a Church that has accepted numerous changes to the text over its nearly two-hundred-year history. What Skousen's work does vividly show, however, is yet another example of the high level of scholarship that has been focused on the book since the late 1970s. It also stands as a stark reminder that although the Church is supportive of academic engagement with the book, Mormon belief is ultimately a matter of faith and divine revelation, not human intelligence.

As Skousen was publishing his multivolume work on the bibliographic intricacies of the 1830 edition of the *Book of Mormon*, publishers outside the Church were beginning to pay unprecedented attention to Mormonism's signature text. In the first decade of the twenty-first century, three non-Mormon publishers produced separate editions of the book in rather rapid succession. In 2003, the University of Illinois Press published Grant Hardy's *The Book of Mormon: A Reader's Edition*, a text bent on offering the book that had been widely available to readers for decades in a more accessible format. Using the 1920 version (because it is in the public domain and outside the control of the Church), Hardy reformatted his *Reader's Edition* "in accordance with the editorial style of most modern editions of the Bible," offering readers a single-column format, paragraphs, poetic stanzas, quotation marks, and content headings. Hardy also included a wide array of apparatus such as explanatory footnotes, pictures, historical charts, an appendix on significant changes in the text over time, a map, diagrams, and a glossary of names to help new and old readers more easily engage with the text.

Another edition that shared Hardy's ideas of reformatting the book for ease of use was published in 2004 by Doubleday with the blessing of the LDS Church. The Church granted Doubleday permission to use its authorized 1981 version of the text and present it in a manner more accessible to those unfamiliar with the book. Doubleday wished to simplify the presentation of the immensely complex narrative, and the Church hoped that the book might find distribution outlets outside its traditional institutional networks through being placed on the bookshelves of stores like Barnes & Noble and in the inventories of online sellers like Amazon.com.

Finally, in 2008 Penguin Publishing produced an academic edition of the *Book of Mormon* (based on the 1840 edition, because it was the last version personally edited by Joseph). Penguin was interested in providing an edition specifically targeted to the collegiate market, as scholars in a number of disciplines, including literature, history, and religious studies, showed increasing interest in the book as an agent of influence in American history. Penguin commissioned the non-Mormon religious studies scholar Laurie Maffly-Kipp to edit the volume to place amid its early American literature offerings.[21] Thus the book joined works by Thoreau, Hawthorne, Melville, and Dickinson in Penguin's much-respected early American literature catalog, gaining its credentials as a text worthy of academic study. Maffly-Kipp's Penguin edition is but one sign of just how far the book has come among American academics. By the early twenty-first century it was finally escaping the narrow confines of Mormon/non-Mormon religious debate as it increasingly came to be treated as an important text in American culture more generally.

Along with Penguin, other academic presses had begun to notice the text. In 2002, Oxford University Press released Terryl L. Givens's *By the Hand of Mormon: The American Scripture That Launched a New World Religion*.[22] The first modern book-length treatment of the *Book of Mormon* by a non-Mormon academic press, Givens's *By the Hand of Mormon* set the tone for a number of scholarly books that would follow as it sidestepped traditional believer/non-believer rubrics for discussion to concentrate instead on the book's culturally formative role both inside and outside Mormonism. Especially important among this new breed of academic book is Grant Hardy's *Understanding the Book of Mormon: A Reader's Guide* (Oxford University Press, 2010), which stands as the first extended attempt to analyze the book's narrative structure as a whole. Hardy's approach is rooted in modern academic theories of narratology, not time-worn discussions of religious veracity.[23] Even this volume from Princeton University Press is yet one more example of the growing academic attention being focused on the *Book of Mormon*.

Although these books differ in their academic approaches and scholarly conclusions, the recent outpouring of university press books on the *Book of Mormon* signals an important shift in the ground where discussions of the book are taking place. For decades treatments of the book have largely fallen into two camps: Mormon educational and apologetic texts and Evangelical works attacking the book's veracity. The *Book of Mormon* has now emerged as a legitimate focal point of academic study. More than simply a text that inspires religious devotion or incites equally religious denunciations, it has come into the current century as a book recognized for its historical role in framing, forming, and fracturing various American cultural beliefs and practices. It has thus taken its place on a larger stage as a book that has transcended its religious roots to become—in the words of Gordon Wood, renowned emeritus professor of American history at Brown University—"one of the greatest documents in American cultural history."[24]

Illustrating the Book

Ezra Taft Benson's clarion call to place the *Book of Mormon* front and center in Mormon life bespoke, among other things, his desire to see more emphasis placed on vivifying the great themes and characters of the book in art, film, drama, literature, and music.[1] To be sure, the book had not been entirely absent in the arts. For example, the Saints already enjoyed a century-long tradition of its painters' representing various scenes from the book. Such representations often found their greatest popularity as they were reproduced to illustrate books on the *Book of Mormon* and even editions of the *Book of Mormon* itself.

The first illustrated version of the text was George Reynolds's *The Story of the Book of Mormon* (1888). If Reynolds is remembered today, it is either because of his impressive work in completing the first exhaustive concordance of the *Book of Mor-*

mon in 1899 or because he stood as the focal point of the 1878 Supreme Court case that forced the LDS Church to retreat from its practice of plural marriage.[2] A personal secretary to Brigham Young, Reynolds acquiesced in Young's request that he offer himself up as the test case to strike down the Morrill Anti-Bigamy Act of 1862. On freedom-of-religion grounds, Young was convinced that the Court would find polygamy an allowable practice. He was wrong. The Court decided against Reynolds, giving him a two-year sentence for his multiple marriages and thereby immortalizing him in Mormon circles as an inspiring prisoner of conscience, a principled man willing to be jailed for his faith. What is far less well known about Reynolds is his having spearheaded the creation of the first illustrated version of the *Book of Mormon*. The importance of this accomplishment, much like his appearance before the Supreme Court, would reverberate throughout the Church for decades to come.

Upon his release from prison in 1881, Reynolds pursued his lifelong passion of educating the Church's young, a love that led him to become intimately involved with the Church's Sunday School movement and the Church's main youth periodical, the *Juvenile Instructor*.[3] After Orson Pratt's death in 1881, many came to consider Reynolds the Church's preeminent scholar on the *Book of Mormon*.[4] Reynolds's friends urged him to combine his scholarship with his educational interests to create a more accessible version of the book for the Church's children. The result was *The Story of the Book of Mormon*, a work in which Reynolds had done a masterful job of simplifying the *Book of Mormon*'s story line and language. It quickly became a standard text in the Church's Sunday School program.[5]

Reynolds was immensely proud of the fact that his book was "the first attempt made to illustrate the Book of Mormon."[6] For his volume, he commissioned forty-two illustrations from four local Utah artists: George M. Ottinger, William T. Armitage, John Held, and W. C. Morris.[7] These men could not have foreseen that their artwork would set the course for hundreds, if not thousands, of future visual imaginings of the *Book of Mormon,* primarily by placing the book's story in various Mesoamerican settings.

To look at *The Story*'s illustrations is to become convinced that Reynolds and his artists were fully aware of the ways in which the Church's leadership had long linked the ancient civilizations discovered in Central America to the narrative translated from the golden plates. As early as 1842, the Church's official newspaper, the *Times and Seasons*, proclaimed that the important Nephite city of Zarahemla was, in fact, located in "Central America, or Guatimala."[8]

Later, Orson Pratt codified such geographical thinking in the footnotes to his 1879 *Book of Mormon* edition, offering his readers such textual glosses as the assertion that "the Land of Nephi" mentioned in the Book of Omni was "supposed to have been in or near Ecuador, South America."[9] Although official Church pronouncements differed, by the 1880s Mormon tradition placed the geography of *Book of Mormon* events in southern Mexico near the present-day borders of Belize and Guatemala.

The Story's illustrations everywhere linked Mesoamerica to the *Book of Mormon*. Five of the volume's first seven illustrations are referenced as "ancient Aztec" charts that hieroglyphically depict Lehi's travels.[10] Reynolds had adapted these charts from the work of one of southern Mexico's first European historians, the eighteenth-century Spaniard Lorenzo Borturini Bernaducci (1702–1753). Borturini had spent eight years in the region then known as New Spain and while there had gathered a massive collection of paintings, maps, and written records. Reynolds had taken images from this collection—made accessible to him through reproductions of the famed Borturini Codex—and gave them his own subtitles. For example, what Borturini had identified as an Aztec image, Reynolds told his readers was a picture of Lehi traveling to a new promised land.

ANCIENT AZTEC CHART SHOWING LEHI'S TRAVELS. NO. 1.

Aztec map as inspired and retitled from the Borturini Codex in George Reynolds's *The Story of the Book of Mormon*.

Along with these charts, Reynolds used other images that clearly referenced Mesoamerican culture in their settings, architecture, and dress. At *The Story's* outset, Reynolds notes that the great challenge to illustrating his book was the almost complete "absence of information in the Book of Mormon of the dress and artificial surroundings of the peoples whose history it recounts."[11] To overcome this obstacle, Reynolds set a precedent in Mormon representational art of portraying scenes from the book in ways that thoroughly mixed ancient Jewish and Mesoamerican culture. Later, in an advertisement soliciting further pictures depicting *Book of Mormon* events, Reynolds told artists that they must pursue historical accuracy by making their characters "Israelites of the sixth century before Christ, and the localities are Palestine, Arabia and Chili [Chile]."[12]

Just one example of Reynolds's penchant for combining ancient Jewish and Mesoamerican culture is seen in George Ottinger's illustration entitled *Destruction of Zarahemla*.[13] Ottinger, a man who had twice been commissioned to paint portraits of Brigham Young and whose *The Baptism of Limhi* (1872) is considered by many to be the first formal painting composed of a *Book of Mormon* subject, produced five images for Reynolds's *Story*.[14] His *Destruction of Zarahemla* is representative of the Mesoamerican overtones that pervade the book. The illustration is full of Central American imagery, perhaps most strikingly seen in the picture's architecture and teetering pre-Columbian totem. (The totem is unmistakably similar to the elaborately carved stone idol Frederick Catherwood had drawn as a frontispiece for John Stephens's *Incidents of Travel in Central America, Chiapas and Yucatan*.)[15] In this picture, and in others, Ottinger demonstrated what would become a common Mormon artistic practice of visualizing the *Book of Mormon* in distinct ancient Central American settings.

Destruction of Zara-
hemla as pictured in
George Reynolds's
*The Story of the Book
of Mormon.*

Stone idol illustration
that served as a frontis-
piece in John L.
Stephens's *Incidents
of Travel in Central
America, Chiapas
and Yucatan.*

It is important to remember amid *The Story's* illustrative links to ancient Mexico that Reynolds envisioned his book as an educative tool for the young. He illustrated *The Story* with the hope that its pictures would draw young readers more deeply into the story. What is remarkable in the decades to follow is just how faithful later *Book of Mormon* storybooks remained to Reynolds's Mesoamerican illustrative vision. Examples are too numerous to list here, but include such widely circulated works as Genet Bingham Dee's *A Voice from the Dust: A Sacred History of Ancient Americans* (1939) and the sixteen-volume *Illustrated Stories from the Book of Mormon* by Clinton Larson that appeared in the 1960s and 1970s.[16] Such volumes are filled with images that continue the Reynoldsian tradition of using ancient Central America as a backdrop for the *Book of Mormon's* story.

Other artists followed Reynolds's lead in illustrating the *Book of Mormon*. Certainly one of the most impressive among this number was Minerva Teichert (1888–1976). Raised on a farm in Idaho, Teichert later trained at the Chicago Art Institute and the Art Students' League in New York City. While in art school, Teichert was once asked whether anyone had "ever painted that great Mormon story of yours?" Her response was simple: "Not to suit me."[17] She set out to change this situation by dedicating nearly thirty years of her life to bringing "the book to life," painting forty-two massive murals and a number of smaller pieces.[18] Beginning her work in 1949, she painted many scenes from the book that are seldom, if ever, artistically rendered.[19] Her contribution to visualizing the *Book of Mormon* was immense both in scope and in artistic quality.

At first glance, mural painting might seem an odd choice of medium for Teichert's work. Teichert, however, wanted to expose as many people as possible to the *Book of Mormon* through her art, and mural painting was used in the United States throughout the 1930s and 1940s as a way to bring art to the people. During these years, federal and state governments commissioned dozens of artists to paint murals to decorate a wide range of public buildings, including schools, courthouses, post offices, and train stations. Such murals made art accessible to large groups of people as they spent time in these public spaces. In this spirit, Teichert envisioned her murals as missionary tools capable of exposing casual viewers from all walks of life to the *Book of Mormon*.[20] Although she was never offered a formal commission for her *Book of Mormon* murals, she painted them anyway, convinced that the time would come when they would find a home where they might educate the world.[21] Today they are housed, but not all displayed, in the collections of the Brigham Young University Museum of Art.

Teichert is unique among Mormon artists not only in her choice of medium, but in her style as well. While religious artists have a long history of favoring realism to portray spiritual themes, Teichert pursued a more impressionist style. Religious artists often use realism to paint spiritual ideas because such a style seems best suited to underline the truth, or the historical veracity, of the scenes portrayed. Other worldly themes are made more accessible through a realist touch. Teichert took her own religious art in a different direction. She believed her impressionist style to be more emotive, and thus better able to capture the emotional truth underlying a given textual moment. Her impressionist approach, however, never signified a cavalier attitude in her approach to the text. She was a serious student of the *Book of Mormon* and saw her art as attempting to capture the core emotional essence of each scene she painted.[22]

Teichert also stands out among Mormon artists because of her firm commitment to bringing forward the female elements of the book, carefully evoking the story's feminine side. Examples abound in her work. Depicting, in *Helaman's Striplings*, the famous scene in Alma when two thousand Lamanite men gather for battle under Helaman's leader-

Minerva Teichert (1888–1976), *Treachery of Amalickiah*,
1950–51, oil on masonite, 35 15/16 × 48 inches. Many of
Teichert's illustrations of *Book of Mormon* scenes focused
on feminine and maternal aspects of the text, as seen here
when she adds children to the story where none are present
in the actual book. Courtesy of Brigham Young University
Museum of Art. All Rights Reserved

ship, she includes the mothers of these young warriors embracing their sons before their departure.
What many Mormon artists typically portray as
men marching forth in the cause of righteousness
is given a distinctly softer touch as Teichert makes
clear the connection between mothers and their
sons.[23] A similar theme is found in her mural titled

Treachery of Amalickiah. Here, the evil Amalickiah stands before his queen, lying about the death of her husband, a man he helped murder. The queen is flanked on either side by her children, a maternal detail nowhere found in the actual text.[24] Both these murals offer a glimpse of Teichert's commitment to exalting the role of women in the *Book of Mormon*.

As impressive and unique as was Teichert's illustrative work on the *Book of Mormon*, her massive corpus of paintings went largely unrecognized within the Church until the 1990s. Particularly important for raising the profile of her work were John Welch and Doris Dant, whose book on Teichert allowed an unprecedented view of the scope of her contribution to Mormon art.[25] Prior to this recognition, when it came to illustrating scenes from the *Book of Mormon*, the Church had shown a clear preference for work that stood at the opposite end of the spectrum from Teichert's: paintings that were both realistic in style and hypermasculine in theme.

Perhaps the clearest example of these masculine, realist preferences is found in the 1963 edition of the *Book of Mormon*. This edition was widely circulated in a blue paperback cover, sporting an iconic image of a golden statue of the angel Moroni. The Church chose to accent this bold new cover design with nineteen interior images, making it the first Church-sanctioned illustrated edition of the text. With this blue-backed edition, a new era in *Book of Mormon* publishing had arrived.

The 1963 edition proved a watershed moment for *Book of Mormon* illustrations in two regards. First, five of the eleven illustrations placed before the actual text of the book unabashedly pointed to the connection between Central America and the book. These five images ranged from depictions of gold plates crafted in Peru to an "Egyptian-like

Images such as this one of Monte Alban, highlighting the connection between Mormonism and Mesoamerica, filled the early pages of the 1963 edition of the *Book of Mormon*. Courtesy of the Church Archives, The Church of Jesus Christ of Latter-day Saints

mural found on temple walls in Mexico" to a panoramic view of the 800 BCE ruins discovered on Monte Alban in Oaxaca Mexico.[26] Monte Alban was the home of an advanced pre-Columbian civilization that was the subject of a great deal of archaeological interest throughout the 1960s. Inspired by advances in pre-Columbian archaeology in general and the work of Thomas Ferguson's New World Archaeological Foundation in particular, the Church reached a new level of comfort and confidence in connecting the *Book of Mormon* to Mesoamerica through the 1963 edition's illustrations.

Second, the 1963 edition included illustrations that imaginatively reproduced several scenes in the book's narrative for the first time. Eight paintings by Arnold Friberg (1913–2010) were placed throughout the edition. Friberg, an artist of such talent that he had won multiple national art awards before graduating high school, had attended the Chicago Academy of Fine Arts. There he gained professional training that he soon put to use as a commercial artist and magazine illustrator. He was so successful that he was eventually invited to train under the renowned Harvey Dunn at the Grand Central School of Art in New York City. Dunn had trained Norman Rockwell, among countless other important magazine illustrators. After serving in World War II, Friberg made excellent use of this training by carving out an artistic niche for himself as one of the nation's foremost painters of religious scenes.[27]

Friberg long believed that God had set him apart to paint in the service of the Church. Passionate about this divine calling, he wished to paint the life of Joseph Smith in a series of forty paintings, and thereby "build Joseph into an American hero."[28] Much to his regret, the Church showed no interest in this idea. Throughout his life, Friberg remained deeply disappointed that the Church had rejected his proposed Joseph project, and commented near his death at age ninety-six that the missed opportunity never ceased to feel like a "knife through me."[29]

In the early 1950s, Adele Cannon Howells, the general president of the Church's Primary School Program for the young (a midweek set of educational classes offered to supplement the Church's regular Sunday School courses), approached Friberg with a commission that would eventually immortalize his art within the pages of the *Book of Mormon*.[30] With her own money and under her own authority, Howells commissioned Friberg to paint twelve pictures to illustrate the *Book of Mormon*. She wished to include the pictures as a special feature in the Church's youth periodical *Children's Friend*, in celebration of the magazine's fiftieth anniversary in 1953, to give young Mormons vivid renderings of the *Book of Mormon*'s great heroes and

Arnold Friberg had a difficult time finding models for his dramatic renderings of scenes from the *Book of Mormon*, so he grew a beard, let his hair grow out, and used himself as a model for his paintings. Courtesy of the Church Archives, The Church of Jesus Christ of Latter-day Saints

momentous events. Friberg quickly accepted the commission, seeing Howells's offer as his chance—denied to him in his Joseph project—to render Mormon history in all its heroic, epic glory. He did not disappoint.

Although he would not complete his paintings in time to have them all included in the 1953 installments of the *Children's Friend*, he did eventually

CHAPTER 7

complete the series by the early 1960s. The principal reason for his delay was that in the midst of his work for Howells, Friberg was invited by Cecil B. DeMille to work on costume and set design for his upcoming movie, *The Ten Commandments* (1956).[31] The Church leadership encouraged Friberg to put aside the Howells commission for a time, seeing that his work on DeMille's movie might prove profitable in enhancing his reputation and possibly providing evangelistic opportunities for the Church. His association with DeMille did, in fact, give him an international audience. Among the many pieces he completed for the movie were fifteen monumental publicity paintings that toured with *The Ten Commandments* "on every inhabited continent."[32] By working with DeMille, Friberg had indeed taken another step to solidify his position as the United States' premier artist of religion.

In response to Friberg's newfound international reputation, the Church decided to include eight of his paintings as illustrations in its new 1963 edition of the *Book of Mormon*. Leaders were particularly drawn to Friberg's realistic rendering of *Book of Mormon* scenes, as well as his ability to add an epic, quasi-mythic quality to his depictions. Perhaps no painting better captures Friberg's mythic aspirations than his *Mormon Bids Farewell to a Once Great Nation*. Here, as Mormon lies dying in the arms of his son, Moroni, both men scan a desolate horizon. Their expansive field of vision underscores their singular place in human history; they alone among the Nephites survey and lament the vast wasteland before them. Friberg further reinforces the epic nature of the scene by placing a markedly strange helmet on Moroni's head. Deviating from the long-standing Mormon artistic practice of dressing ancient Nephite warriors in either Roman or Mesoamerican military garb, Friberg chooses to mix Roman and Scandanavian motifs, thereby invoking the great tradition of the Norse saga. (Friberg was a great admirer of Richard Wagner's operas and found inspiration for his *Mormon Bids Farewell* in Wagner's portrayal of the Norse hero Siegfried in his *The Ring of the Nibelung* operatic series.)[33] Just as such sagas immortalized early Viking voyages and countless Icelandic blood feuds, Friberg enshrines the last two survivors of the once-proud, and now totally destroyed, Nephite civilization.

Friberg's paintings are also notable for how they capture the gender politics of the *Book of Mormon*'s narrative. A profoundly masculine text, its story is full of mighty men and mightier battles, while referring by name to only five female characters in the course of its some six hundred pages. Friberg's most dominant figures are unfailingly men, and almost all of them could have stepped out of the pages of

Mormon Bids Farwell to a Once Great Nation by Arnold Friberg. Friberg mixed epic Roman and Norse styles to create his own mythic characterizations of *Book of Mormon* figures. Here, Mormon cradles the plates he has so carefully edited for future generations while his son cradles him. Courtesy of the Church Archives, The Church of Jesus Christ of Latter-day Saints

a superhero comic book. His work is full of stalwart heroes who confront the most dangerous situations with imposing physical presence and an unflinching gaze. In *Nephi Subdues His Rebellious Brothers* Friberg paints Nephi as a man who appears larger than life. For Friberg, this was no accident. He wished to render his paintings realistic in detail, but then to enlarge the composition of his principal characters. Thus Friberg painted such key figures as Nephi,

Alma, Ammon, and Captain Moroni in a hypermasculine, almost superhuman fashion, explaining that "[t]he muscularity in my paintings is only an expres-

Nephi Subdues His Rebellious Brothers by Arnold Friberg. This representation of Nephi grew so popular that it later became the only way to picture Nephi in many Mormon circles. Courtesy of the Church Archives, The Church of Jesus Christ of Latter-day Saints

CHAPTER 7

sion of the spirit within . . . I'm painting the interior, the greatness, the largeness of spirit." In commenting on his depiction of Nephi, he stated: "Who knows what he looked like? I'm painting a man who looks like he could actually do what Nephi did."[34]

In the coming years, the Church's choice of illustrations for its editions of the book would continue to mirror the masculine emphasis of the narrative, but the linkages of the text to Mesoamerica would diminish through subtle and not-so-subtle changes. By the late 1970s, when no hard archaeological evidence had appeared in southern Mexico to link the book's events to that part of the world, the Church became more reluctant to tie the book so directly to Mesoamerica. In 1981, the Church released its newly revised edition of the *Book of Mormon* without photographic illustrations of artifacts and ruins that explicitly fused Mesoamerica to the text. Even with this move away from formal linkages between the book and the region, it is interesting to note that ties between the two continued to be reflected in the artistic images that the Church did include in the 1981 edition. Such images still pointed— although in less direct ways—to the book's pre-Columbian connections by using Mesoamerican flourishes in how they represented the story's settings, as seen in such pictures as John Scott's popular *Jesus Christ Visits the Americas*.

John Scott's *Jesus Christ Visits the Americas* follows in the
tradition of portraying *Book of Mormon* events in Central
American settings. *Jesus Christ Visits the Americas* by John
Scott © Intellectual Reserve, Inc.

While Church leaders decreased the number
of illustrations they chose to include in the single-
volume edition of the *Book of Mormon* (from nineteen illustrations in the 1963 edition to just eight in
the 1981 edition), a marked rise in the use of *Book
of Mormon* illustrations can be seen in other books
connected to the text. This increase is particularly noticeable in a plethora of *Book of Mormon*–
centered children's books that began to be published in the 1980s as computer technology made

such highly illustrated books less expensive to produce. Although Friberg's realism is seldom replicated in this new wave of children's books—they are often drawn in a cartoon style—the Reynoldsian illustrative connection between the *Book of Mormon* and Mesoamerica remains firm. Examples abound, including more recent titles like Deanna Draper Buck's *My First Book of Mormon Stories* (2001), Kimberly Jensen Bowman's *Jr. Book of Mormon: A Pictorial Study-Guide for Children* (2001), and David Bowman's *Who's Your Greatest Hero? Jesus Visits the Nephites* (2009).[35] While the Church may take no official stance on where events in the *Book of Mormon* took place, Mormon children learn at a young age from literature produced by, and for, Mormons that there is likely a connection between their religion's founding text and the past civilizations of southern Mexico and Central America.

Perhaps one of the most recent and most vivid fusions of themes to be found in Mormon illustrative practice is Michael Allred's *Book of Mormon* comic book series, *The Golden Plates*. Allred, most famous for his work on the independent *Madman* comic book series, advertises his series as "The Book of Mormon in Pictures and Word." Underlining the fact that art is never created in a vacuum, Allred's comic books show their indebtedness to decades of Mormon art. Volumes of *The Golden Plates* are

The Golden Plates comic book series is just one of dozens of modern attempts to visualize the *Book of Mormon*. Courtesy of AAA Pop Comics

filled with muscular men, an emphasis on the masculine nature of the book, and allusions to the *Book of Mormon*'s Mesoamerican connections.[36] Along with populating his book with Fribergian heroic figures, Allred carefully includes pictures of pre-Columbian architecture, as well as maps that show the story's central action taking place in the southern Mexican region that John Sorenson, among others, has selected as the likely home of *Book of Mormon* events.[37]

That Allred chose to render the *Book of Mormon* in comic book form also shows a sensitivity to market forces, as comic-based visual art has become commonplace in everything from video games to Hollywood blockbuster movies like *Batman*, *X-Men*, and *Captain America*. As the presence and profile of the *Book of Mormon* have risen within the LDS Church, its members have looked for ways to engage readers outside the Church with its message. Allred's *Golden Plates* is a prime example of such an evangelistic endeavor. His comic books include extended apologetic discourses on the inside of their front and back covers to help "persuade the reader to the intellectual truth and authenticity of *The Book of Mormon*."[38] While Allred's comic books have met with limited success in non-Mormon circles, other art forms have proved more popular. In particular, various dramatic renderings of the book have enjoyed greater success beyond strictly Mormon audiences. It is to these dramatic forms that we now turn.

The Book on Screen and Stage

Artistic renderings of the *Book of Mormon* have not been confined to the pages of books and artists' oil paintings. Various dramatic representations of the book have been produced over the years, on both the screen and the stage. As early as 1915, the Church embraced the new technology of film to tell the book's story. In that year, the First Presidency granted permission to William A. Morton, an active member of the Church's General Board of Religion Classes, to make the first feature film based on the *Book of Mormon*.[1] Morton saw film as a great tool to educate both Mormons and non-Mormons alike concerning the book, and he even planned to produce an illustrated edition of the *Book of Mormon* that would use images from his motion picture to accompany the sacred text.[2]

Morton first attempted to work with two young filmmakers, Chet and Shirl Clawson, to bring the *Book of Mormon* to the screen. Although the Clawson brothers would be vitally important to later Mormon filmmaking, they proved financially unable to pursue Morton's vision.[3] Morton then turned to Anton J. T. Sorensen and William J. Burns, men who had both an interest in motion pictures and the financial resources to help him complete the film. Their film, *The Life of Nephi*, appeared in October 1915. Sadly, all copies of the film have been lost. Only a few stills, which were used in

The silent motion picture *The Life of Nephi* (1915) was the first attempt to bring the *Book of Mormon* to the silver screen. Courtesy of the Church Archives, The Church of Jesus Christ of Latter-day Saints

magic lantern shows to help promote the film, now remain to give a glimpse of this production.

The Life of Nephi signals in its title alone a reality that has marked every subsequent film adaptation of the book: namely, the *Book of Mormon* is too large and complex a story to be captured in a single motion picture. *The Life of Nephi* covered only the initial stories found in the *Book of Mormon* concerning Lehi and his family fleeing Jerusalem and arriving in their new home across the ocean.[4] Beginning with Sorensen and Burns, filmmakers have been forced to make a decision when attempting to bring the book to the silver screen: they must either envision multifilm projects to tell the book's story, or settle for focusing on a single narrative moment around which to build a motion picture. Morton had wished *The Life of Nephi* to be the first of a series of movies that would tell the book's story, but it was, unfortunately, the only installment ever made.

The next motion picture to take the *Book of Mormon* as its topic pursued the strategy of presenting only a single portion of the book's narrative. In 1931, Lester Park released *Corianton: A Story of Unholy Love*, an ambitious feature-length film based on a theatrical adaptation of a 1889 story published by B. H. Roberts, one of the Church's most noted historians and *Book of Mormon* scholars.[5] Park had high hopes for the film, as it presented a quasi-

The film *Corianton* was not officially endorsed by the Church of Jesus Christ of Latter-day Saints, but the Church did allow its famous Tabernacle Choir to play a role in the production. Courtesy L. Tom Perry Special Collections, Harold B. Lee Library, Brigham Young University

biblical story full of sex and violence. Inspired by similar historical epics that had been blockbusters at the box office, such as Cecil B. DeMille's first, silent, version of *The Ten Commandments* (1923) and Fred Niblo's *Ben-Hur* (1925), Park advertised the movie as "a worthy successor to Ben-Hur" and believed that *Corianton* could command large audiences and thus large revenues.[6]

Park was further encouraged by the fact that he could improve upon the work of DeMille and Niblo by making *Corianton* an "all talking movie."[7] He wished it to be the film to usher the biblical epic out of the silent era. With the promise of sound, Park gained permission from the Church to use the already-famous Mormon Tabernacle Choir to perform the movie's music. He also enlisted Dr. Edgar Stillman-Kelly, the man who had composed the music for a wildly popular Broadway adaptation of Lew Wallace's *Ben-Hur* (1899), to compose an original movie score.[8] To capitalize on Kelly's work, Park filled his film with elaborately choreographed scenes including dozens of dancers. The film stands as the first high-profile, commercial adaption of the *Book of Mormon*. It also turned out to be a massive financial failure.[9]

The film liberally adapts a small portion of the Book of Alma to provide the backbone of the film's basic narrative. In the adaptation, Corianton, a follower of the Antichrist figure Korihor, repents when he sees God strike Korihor dead with a lightning bolt. Corianton then uses his newfound faith to aid his brother in spreading the Gospel among the Zoramites. Corianton, however, is seduced by the Zoramite harlot, Zoan Ze Isobel. The stories that fill the *Book of Mormon* are almost entirely devoid of sex and romance, so the seductress Isobel ("Isabel" in the actual *Book of Mormon*) provided Roberts, and those who followed him in dramatizing the tale, with a rare opportunity to expose the dangers of sexual sin. No doubt the story's mix of religion and sex appealed to those who chose to dramatize it first on the stage and

The 1931 motion picture *Corianton: A Story of Unholy Love* was filmed before Hollywood instituted its rigorous production code and thus proved too salacious for Mormon audiences. In this picture, Corianton (played by Eric Alden) begins to regret his relationship with the barely clad seductress Zoan Ze Isobel (played by Theo Pennington). Courtesy L. Tom Perry Special Collections, Harold B. Lee Library, Brigham Young University

then on the screen, but it was also largely the film's strong sexual aspect that doomed it to failure.

When the film was offered in limited release for six weeks in Utah, it was too salacious for its Mormon audience. Completed before the Hayes Production Code had been established, the film is filled with scantily clad women, many of them promiscuously undulating in the orgy scene where Corianton falls under Isobel's spell. As the film progresses, Isobel often keeps her clothing to a minimum as she continues her seductive relationship with Corianton. The film could not find an audience in Utah or outside it, and it quietly slipped into obscurity. So low was the film's profile that for many years it was believed that Park had never even completed it. In 2005, Park's daughters donated to Brigham Young University a 16 mm copy of the picture that the family had stored for decades in a Washington State barn, offering conclusive proof that Park had indeed finished the first talking motion picture adaptation of the *Book of Mormon*.

After *Corianton*, attempts to make film versions of the *Book of Mormon* were for decades less ambitious. For various instructional and evangelistic purposes, the Church has produced shorter films of the book, such as *The Testaments of One Fold and One Shepherd* (2007), and vignettes of the book have appeared at times in other Mormon films such as *How Rare a Possession: The Book of Mormon* (1987), but the dream of making a full-length feature film adaption of the book lay largely dormant for almost three-quarters of a century after the appearance of *Corianton*.[10] In 2001, Gary Rogers, a successful Mormon television producer, embarked on the hugely ambitious project of bringing the entire book to the screen in what he believed would eventually be a mammoth eight- or nine-film series.

Inspired—like Park before him—by Cecil B. DeMille, Rogers believed that the time was finally right to give the public a stunning adaption of the *Book of Mormon* that might rival the evocative religious power and box office popularity of DeMille's 1956 *The Ten Commandments*.[11] Convinced that special effects technology had evolved to the point where the book's monumental narrative could be brought to the screen in a compelling way, Rogers set out to produce a film that would attract a Church audience that had grown large enough to constitute a viable, even lucrative, motion picture market. He was convinced that Church members were eager to see a motion picture made of their religion's signature text.

Rogers pursued the project with single-minded devotion, and in September 2003 released *The Book of Mormon Movie, Vol. 1: The Journey*. He had chosen to make a film that closely followed the *Book of*

Mormon's story. So *The Journey* is a rendering of the book's opening stories as found in the First and Second Books of Nephi. In deference to his anticipated largely Mormon audience, Rogers put together a film that treated the *Book of Mormon*'s narrative in a highly literal way. Just as the Church's translation department has remained committed to rendering the text as closely as possible to the most currently endorsed English version of the book, Rogers pursued narrative accuracy (archaic language and all) with equal vigor. Much of the film's dialogue is taken directly from the *Book of Mormon*'s actual wording, full of King Jamesian "thee"s and "thou"s.

Rogers was equally careful when it came to casting his movie. Mindful that many in his audience would have definite ideas as to what certain characters might look like, he purposefully chose actors and actresses who looked like the men and women in the Arnold Friberg illustrations that had graced the pages of the *Book of Mormon* for nearly forty years. Rogers thus cast Noah Danby in the lead role of Nephi in part because Danby so strongly resembled Friberg's iconic representation of Nephi.

Rogers's safe, literalist approach doomed his movie. What may work in textual translation does not always succeed in the attempt to render an immensely complex, biblically styled book into a film. Along with offering its audience dialogue in the archaic-sounding language of the *Book of Mormon*, the movie attempted to follow the story of Nephi in a way that too closely adhered to the text. As a result, the movie is little more than a series of episodes that portray two-dimensional characters moving quickly, but not always coherently, from one scene to another. The film lacks any larger sense of narrative momentum, climax, or resolution. What works in the episodic genre of sacred literature does not automatically make for good cinema.

The Journey makes it abundantly clear why De-Mille took certain narrative liberties in making *The Ten Commandments*. DeMille felt free to add characters and plot action in order to offer his viewers a central story built around a version of Moses that showed his foibles, flaws, and a sense of self-awareness leading to growth. *The Journey* gives its leading character, Nephi, none of these elements and thereby forgoes offering viewers a dynamic, engaging protagonist. Nephi is the same at the end of the movie as he is at the beginning, and the stories he woodenly strides through are strung together in such a fashion that one is hard-pressed to care much about any one episode or any one character. One reviewer found the movie so boring that he parodied Mark Twain's famous characterization of the *Book of Mormon* by calling Rogers's motion picture "chloroform on film."[12] In the end, *The Journey* did not live up to Rogers's grand vision. The film barely recouped its production costs, dooming any hope that the series's second installment, *Zarahemla*, would ever be made.[13]

In an age where visual drama is dominated by television, computer games, and motion pictures, it is striking that the most successful dramatization of the *Book of Mormon* takes place in none of these media. The most compelling dramatic rendering of the book by Mormons is a pageant, harking back to a theatrical form popular in the nineteenth and early twentieth centuries but rarely seen in today's world of entertainment. Inspired by a local pageant staged by the Brooklyn Branch of the Church in May 1936 entitled *Truth from the Earth* and an opulent four-million-dollar non-Mormon Broadway show about Jewish history, *The Eternal Road* (1937), a group of Mormons located in upstate New York decided to stage their own pageant, on the Hill Cumorah in 1937, *America's Witness for Christ*.[14] This pageant came to be more commonly known as the Hill Cumorah Pageant, and for Mormons this spectacle is the equivalent to the magnificent Passion Play presented once every decade in Oberammergau, Germany.[15]

Pageants are an art form that the LDS Church has kept alive since the early twentieth century, and their performances have become an important part of Mormon culture. Currently, the Church sponsors seven pageants, located from California to New York. Not every pageant focuses as directly on the *Book of Mormon* as the one staged at the Hill Cumorah, but all have become important sites of Mormon pilgrimage. Mormons flock to these pageants to reaffirm and testify to their faith. It is considered a great honor to act in or work on these dramatizations. Mormons apply for highly competitive pageant positions, and both actors and crew are willing to work eighteen hours a day with no pay, as well as cover their own travel and living costs, just to be involved in a production. There is a sacred communal aspect to the production and performance of these pageants that any motion picture of the *Book of Mormon* would be hard-pressed to capture.

No pageant enjoys greater longevity or prestige than the one held for ten days each July at the Hill Cumorah in upstate New York. By its twenty-fifth anniversary in 1962, *America's Witness for Christ* had grown from an amateur production staged by a few local Mormon congregations to an affair that included a million dollars' worth of support buildings, a staging area on Cumorah's hillside the size of a football field, with "25 stages, five miles of underground wiring for lights and sound, reservoirs holding 175,000 gallons of water for the refulgently illuminated water curtains," and a cast of 300 actors.

The Hill Cumorah pageant, with its seven-hundred-person cast, is presented each summer in upstate New York. Here, Lehi holds high the sacred plates of scripture for all to see. Courtesy of Gerald S. Argetsinger

By the turn of the twenty-first century, the spectacle had grown to include more than 700 cast members. Leading roles in the pageant are capable of attracting celebrity acting and singing talent. Donny Osmond played Samuel the Righteous Lamanite in the 1997 show.[16] By the year 2000, it was estimated that 80,000 spectators were traveling annually to see the pageant, and that some 2 million people had seen some version of *America's Witness for Christ* on the Cumorah hillside since its first show in 1937.[17]

CHAPTER 8

The script of the Hill Cumorah Pageant has changed over the years.[18] The first version was written by H. Wayne Driggs, an English professor at New York University. The most recent script is the work of best-selling fantasy and science fiction author Orson Scott Card (the grandson of *Corianton's* Lester Park). In the late 1980s, the Church tasked Card with writing a script that would appeal to "a modern audience, targeting the non-scripture-reading, non-Mormon young adult," reinvigorating the Church's evangelistic vision for the show.[19] In the main, the pageant's story is an intriguing mixture of intertwined narratives that alternate between Joseph's discovery of the plates at the Hill Cumorah and the story he translates from those plates. The stage is largely Mesoamerican in design, and the primary messages of the pageant revolve around the Mormon belief that Jesus Christ once visited the Western Hemisphere, and that the Church of Jesus Christ of Latter-day Saints has restored the true Gospel to the world.

The *Book of Mormon* is a central component both of the pageant's core narrative, and of every activity surrounding its production. Although Mormons largely make up the pageant audiences each evening, many non-Mormons attend as well. Mormon missionaries circulate through the crowds, talking to visitors, collecting inquiry cards that might be followed up later, and distributing copies of the *Book of Mormon*. The book stands at the center of the spectacle in terms of not only the drama's content, but its intent as well. The purpose of the pageant is more than collective celebration and Mormon identity formation; it is an evangelistic tool bent on telling the story of the *Book of Mormon* and inspiring both Mormons and non-Mormons to read the book.

If visual representations of the *Book of Mormon* are intended to engage their audiences more fully with the book itself, perhaps no vehicle outside the illustrations found in various editions of the *Book of Mormon* has succeeded as well as the Hill Cumorah Pageant. In *America's Witness for Christ*, the Church may use an anachronistic dramatic form to visually imagine the text, but the popularity of the form is beyond dispute. On the very hillside where Joseph reportedly first uncovered the golden plates, the Church has been able to recapture some of the dramatic magic of that discovery.

Most recently, dramatic *Book of Mormon* magic has taken the form of a hugely successful Broadway musical named for the book itself. The result of a seven-year collaboration between Trey Parker and Matt Stone, creators of the immensely popular *South Park* television show, and Robert Lopez, cocreator of the *Sesame Street*–warping *Avenue Q*, their musical *The Book of Mormon* opened in March

2011 to almost universal critical acclaim. Theater critics who had been skeptical of a project centered on an exotic book often relegated to the margins of American religion greeted the show with reviews ranging from "Musical-comedy heaven" to "Wildly original, jubilant and expert."[20] By the summer of 2011, the show had won an incredible nine Tony Awards, including Best Musical, and its soundtrack had climbed to the number three spot on Billboard's Top 100 list, becoming the first top-ten Broadway musical soundtrack since 1967's *Hair*.[21]

The musical tells the story of two young male missionaries who are sent to Uganda. Both men have little knowledge of Africa except what they have gleaned from Disney's *The Lion King*. One of these missionaries, Elder Cunningham, hits upon the strategy of inventing stories and adding them to the *Book of Mormon*, hoping that they will thereby engage native Ugandans more successfully with the Mormon Gospel. A series of not-so-subtle parallels interconnect the Elder Cunningham's wild tales (including references to hobbits, the fiery pits of Mordor, and the Death Star) with the stories Joseph supposedly translated from golden plates about Jesus visiting America and Native Americans being of Jewish descent.

The musical is filled with theatrical high jinks, foul language, and reflections on the value of re-

Elder Price (played by Andrew Rannells) stands in the middle alongside Elder Cunningham (played by Josh Gad) as they embark on their mission to Africa in the Broadway musical *The Book of Mormon* (2011). © Joan Marcus; courtesy of Joan Marcus Photography

ligious belief. It also features classic Broadway show-tune music. In a song entitled "All-American Prophet," the missionaries tell their listeners: "You all know the Bible is made of testaments old and new / You've been told it's just those two parts, or only one if you're a Jew."[22] They then go on to proclaim that the *Book of Mormon* is a "fresh third part," a new revelation that makes the Bible into a trilogy of sorts.[23] Ultimately the play tries to teach its audience that religious "prophets ALWAYS speak in met-

CHAPTER 8

aphors," and their divinely inspired texts are most helpful when viewed in symbolic, not literal, ways.[24]

Regardless of its message, the show's extreme popularity and overwhelming critical success signaled that the *Book of Mormon* had finally escaped the confines of strictly religious discourse. No longer a book characterized strictly dualistically—as dangerous and delusional by Evangelicals and Roman Catholics, or sacred and inspiring by Mormons—the *Book of Mormon* had become a topic of conversation beyond such narrow religious circles. Once only a marvelous work and a wonder to its faithful adherents, in recent years the *Book of Mormon* has captured a larger role in both non-Mormon academic discourse and the popular American imagination. Not everyone may believe its contents, but fewer and fewer can continue to doubt the importance the book holds in American history and culture.

Epilogue

I, the Lord, have appointed them, and ordained
them to be stewards over the revelations and
commandments which I have given unto them,
and which I shall hereafter give unto them;
And an account of this stewardship will I
require of them in the day of judgment.

—Doctrine and Covenants 70:3–4

Sacred texts are also sacred trusts. In this spirit, Mormons have a long tradition of treating their founding religious text with tremendous care. The leadership of the Church of Jesus Christ of Latter-day Saints (LDS) feels a weighty responsibility to reproduce accurately and distribute passionately a record they believe was passed down through a long line of scribes until it was buried and then recovered by Joseph Smith Jr. in the late 1820s. The book itself testifies to this sacred history of transmission in telling its readers that the ancient prophet Mormon took only "a hundredth part" of the plates at his disposal and wrote a new history for a future time with a special eye to matters that would be relevant in that day.[1] Today's Church leadership carefully guards that one-hundredth part, absolutely convinced that Mormon's record is exactly what today's men and women need to hear in order to be saved.

Such stewardship has taken many forms in recent decades. The Church's leadership, driven by the belief that it will one day be held accountable for how it handled the text, has taken whatever steps it has deemed necessary to protect the integrity of Mormon's message. Most recently, these steps have included an unbending commitment to translating the text as literally as possible rather than modernizing it. The Church is extremely careful when it comes to changing the wording of the text. When changes do occur, they need to be approved at the highest levels of the Church's leadership. These leaders are famously conservative in their textual preferences. They firmly believe that any textual changes can be warranted only by some form of divine guidance, so even the slightest alterations to the book are considered matters of great importance and do not happen quickly. Every change is weighed against a desire to preserve both the spirit and the letter of Mormon's message.

The Church has also ensured the integrity of the text by almost totally centralizing its printing in one location in Salt Lake City. Roughly 90 percent of the Church's production of the *Book of Mormon* takes place at a single printing plant and upon a single giant press at this plant. There are only a handful of exceptions to this centralization, such as the Japanese, Korean, and Chinese editions, which are typeset and printed in Asia. By so centralizing the book's production, the Church is able to control not only the quality of the printed texts, but the production costs as well. As nearly 350,000 copies of the *Book of Mormon* issue forth from this publishing center every month, every detail of the 4 million copies printed annually is closely monitored. Thus the Church's leaders are able to make sure copies of their sacred text meet the most exacting production standards, a level of quality control that would be much more difficult to enforce if they outsourced the book's production to independent, third-party publishing houses.

The LDS Church's leadership has also built several legal hedges around the book. On the most basic level, it has copyrighted the text and holds the licensing rights to any version of the *Book of Mormon* produced by its branch of Mormonism after 1920. (Before this date, editions have entered the public domain and can be reprinted without the permission of the Church.) Less effectively, the Church has trademarked the phrase "Book of Mormon" in an attempt to help ensure that people know what products might have the official endorsement of the Church and what products do not. Trademarking is a means of helping consumers trace the source of a product, and while the Church does not mind descriptive uses of the phrase "Book of Mormon," it is mindful of people who attempt to name products in such a way as to imply Church sponsorship. Such trademarking is one method the LDS Church employs to police the use of the book and its title phrase in wide range of settings. For example, when action figures depicting characters from the *Book of Mormon* appeared in Mormon bookstores, the packaging of these figures never contained the phrase "Book of Mormon." The Church had not sanctioned the product, and thus the product did not invoke the book's name.

Those outside the Church pay less heed to the Church's attempt to trademark the book's title or control the book's content. The Community of Christ has its own versions of the text, and it does not turn to the LDS Church when it wishes to invoke the book's title. Neither did Trey Parker, Robert Lopez, and Matt Stone seek permission to use the book's title when they named their Broadway musical *The Book of Mormon*. In one sense, the

Church's move to trademark the phrase "Book of Mormon" highlights the tension between its desire to steward the text well and the fact that the book is "owned" to an ever greater extent not just by the Church, but by American culture more generally. One need not look any further than *The Book of Mormon* Broadway musical to see the extent to which the book has gained a place independent of the Church in America's popular imagination.

The *Book of Mormon* has become a victim of its own success. As Mormonism grows, so does the world's awareness of it and its signature text. The LDS Church may strive to control the book and even the use of its title, but an ever-growing awareness of the book and its contents has put it beyond the sole dominion of the Church. Still, the ways in which Mormons continue to preserve the integrity of their signature text stand as an impressive testimony not only to the power of divinely inspired writings, but to the measures religious bodies will take to guard uncommon, sacred words when they appear in common, earthly forms.

Notable *Book of Mormon* Editions in English

(In order of appearance)[1]

1830 (March) First printing (5,000 copies) is published by E. B. Grandin of Palmyra, New York.

1837 Second edition (either 3,000 or 5,000 copies) is published at Kirtland Ohio.

1840 Third edition and first stereotyped edition (2,000 copies) is published in Nauvoo, Illinois, and printed in Cincinnati under the direction of Ebenezer Robinson.

1841 First British edition (4,050 copies) is published in Liverpool, England, under the direction of Brigham Young, Heber C. Kimball, and Parley P. Pratt.

1842 New impression of 1840 edition is published in Nauvoo, Illinois.

1849 Second British edition is published in England under the direction of Orson Pratt.

1852	Third British edition, including first use of numbered paragraphs, is published in England under the direction of Franklin D. Richards.
1858	Private edition is published in New York City by James O. Wright.
1874	First RLDS edition is published in Plano, Illinois.
1879	Major LDS edition is published in Salt Lake City and Liverpool under the direction of Orson Pratt, with the text divided into longer chapters and arranged in versification and with footnotes.
1892	Second RLDS edition is published in Lamoni, Iowa, the first edition to use a double-column format.
1902	Missionary LDS edition is published in Kansas City, Missouri.
1908	Third RLDS edition is published in Lamoni, Iowa.
1920	Major LDS edition is published in Salt Lake City under the direction of a committee probably headed by James E. Talmage, the first LDS edition to use double columns.
1953	Current RLDS (now Community of Christ) edition is published in Independence, Missouri.
1966	RLDS Church publishes the New Authorized Version (or "reader's edition") of the *Book of Mormon*, the first attempt to modernize the book and its language.

1981	Major LDS edition is published in Salt Lake City under the direction of a committee headed by members of the Quorum of the Twelve; includes corrections, new introductory material, new chapter summaries, and new footnotes. These additional materials are particularly useful in integrating the content—through study aids and cross references—of the four sacred works of the Church: The *Book of Mormon, Doctrine and Covenants, The Pearl of Great Price,* and the Bible. Increasingly, these books have subsequently been bound together for Church members in Triple (editions of the three major Mormon sacred works without the Bible) and Quad (with the Bible) formats.
1982	Subtitle *Another Testament of Jesus Christ* is added to cover and half-title page in LDS editions (but not to the title page itself).
1988–2007	Supported by the Foundation for Ancient Research and Mormon Studies (FARMS), Royal Skousen produces a comprehensive multivolume critical text project of the 1830 and other important early editions and manuscripts.
2003	University of Illinois Press publishes reader's edition, edited by Grant Hardy; 1920 version is used as base text and reformatted in the manner of modern translations of the Bible.

| 2004 | In partnership with the LDS Church, Doubleday publishes the first official trade edition of the book; 1981 version is used as base text. |

Book of Mormon Translations

(In order of appearance)

Language	First Published	Present Edition
1. English	1830, full book	new 1981
2. Danish	1851, full book	revised 1949, 2005
3. German	1852, full book	revised 2003
4. French	1852, full book	revised 1998
5. Italian	1852, full book	revised 1995
6. Welsh	1852, full book	reprint 2001
7. Hawaiian	1855, full book	reprint 1992
8. Spanish	1875, Selections	full 1886; revised 1992
9. Swedish	1878, full book	revised 1958
10. Maori	1889, full book	reprint 1989
11. Dutch	1890, full book	revised 2004
12. Samoan	1903, full book	
13. Tahitian	1904, full book	
14. Turkish	1906, selections	full book 2001
15. Japanese	1909, full book	revised 2009
16. Czech	1933, full book	revised 2004
17. Armenian-Western	1937, full book	selections 1983
18. Portuguese	1939, full book	revised 1995
19. Tongan	1946, full book	revised 2006
20. Norwegian	1950, full book	revised 2002
21. Finnish	1954, full book	revised 2002

Language	First Published	Present Edition
22. Rarotongan	1965, full book	
23. Chinese	1965, full book	revised 2007
24. Korean	1967, full book	revised 2005
25. Afrikaans	1972, full book	revised 2003
26. Thai	1976, full book	
27. Indonesian	1977, full book	
28. Aymara	1977, selections	full book 1986
29. Cakchiquel	1978, selections	cassettes 2000
30. Croatian	1979, full book	
31. Quechua-Peru	1979, selections	
32. Greek	1979, selections	full book 1987
33. Hungarian	1979, selections	full 1991; revised 2005
34. Kekchi	1979, selections	full 1983; cassettes 2000
35. Quiche	1979, selections	cassettes 2000
36. Bulgarian	1980, selections	full book 2004
37. Navajo	1980, selections	revised 1998; cassettes 2000
38. Quichua-Ecuador	1980, selections	full book, 2011
39. Arabic	1980, selections	full book 1986
40. Vietnamese	1980, selections	full 1982; revised 2003
41. Fijian	1980, full book	
42. Quechua-Bolivia	1981, selections	
43. Russian	1981, full book	
44. Catalan	1981, full book	
45. Polish	1981, full book	
46. Romanian	1981, selections	full book 2004
47. Kuna	1981, selections	
48. Niuean (Niue)	1981, selections	
49. Hebrew	1981, selections	
50. Icelandic	1981, full book	revised 2002
51. Hindi	1982, full book	
52. Telugu	1982, selections	full book 2000
53. Tamil	1982, selections	full book 2005
54. Cambodian	1982, selections	full book 2007
55. Laotian	1982, selections	

Language	First Published	Present Edition
56. Swahili	1982, selections	full book 2005
57. Guarani	1982, selections	full book 2009
58. Maya	1983, selections	
59. Sinhala	1983, selections	full book 2008
60. Mam	1983, selections	cassettes 2000
61. Efik	1983, selections	
62. Chinese (simple char.)	1983, selections	full book 2000
63. Kisii (Gusii)	1983, selections	
64. Hmong	1983, selections	full book 2000
65. Persian (Farsi)	1983, selections	
66. Haitian	1983, selections	full 1999; revised 2007
67. Marshallese	1984, selections	full book 2003
68. Bengali	1985, selections	
69. Bislama	1985, selections	full book 2004
70. Malagasy	1986, selections	full 2000; revised 2006
71. Fante	1987, selections	full book (revised) 2003
72. Zulu	1987, selections	full book 2003
73. Pohnpeian	1987, selections	
74. Papiamento	1987, selections	
75. Chuukese (Trukese)	1987, selections	
76. Tagalog	1987, selections	full book 1998
77. Lingala	1988, selections	full book 2004
78. Shona	1988, selections	full book 2007
79. Urdu	1988, selections	full book 2007
80. Palauan	1988, selections	
81. Kiribati	1988, selections	full book 2001
82. Chamorro	1989, selections	
83. Ilokano	1991, selections	full book 1995
84. Cebuano	1992, selections	full book 1998
85. Tzotzil	1994, selections	cassettes 2000
86. Hiligaynon	1994, selections	full book 2005
87. Pampango	1994, selections	
88. American Sign Lang.	1995–2001, full book, video	DVD 2006
89. Waray	1996, selections	

Language	First Published	Present Edition
90. Ukrainian	1997, full book	revised 2005
91. Bikolano	1998, selections	
92. Pangasinan	1998, full book	
93. Albanian	1999, full book	revised 2005
94. Estonian	2000, full book	
95. Igbo	2000, full book	revised 2007
96. Latvian	2000, full book	revised 2006
97. Armenian-Eastern	2000, full book	revised 2006
98. Lithuanian	2000, full book	revised 2006
99. Amharic	2000, full book	
100. Xhosa	2000, full book	
101. Mongolian	2001, full book	
102. Neomelanesian	2002, full book	
103. Slovenian	2002, full book	
104. Tswana	2003, full book	
105. Yapese	2004, full book	
106. Twi	2005, full book	
107. Yoruba	2007, full book	
108. Serbian	2008, full book	
109. Sinhala	2008, full book	

PROLOGUE

1. Paul C. Gutjahr, *An American Bible: A History of the Good Book in the United States, 1777–1880* (Stanford, CA: Stanford University Press, 1999), 19, 187.

2. Hugh Grant Stocks, "The Book of Mormon, 1830–1879: A Publishing History" (master's thesis, UCLA, 1979), 38.

3. Paul C. Gutjahr, "The Golden Bible in the Bible's Golden Age: *The Book of Mormon* and Antebellum Print Culture," *American Transcendental Quarterly*, n.s., 12:4 (December 1998): 278.

4. A helpful chronology of the *Book of Mormon*'s narrative can be found in Grant Hardy, ed., *The Book of Mormon: A Reader's Edition* (Urbana: University of Illinois Press, 2003), 675–683.

5. *Book of Mormon* (1830), 5.

6. *Book of Mormon* (1830), title page.

7. *Book of Mormon* (1981), 1 Nephi 1:9, 1:19, 10:2–4, 11:33; Enos 1:8; Alma 45:10.

8. *Book of Mormon* (1981), 3 Nephi 11:10.

9. *Book of Mormon* (1981), 3 Nephi 11–27

10. Daniel Walker Howe, *What Hath God Wrought: The Transformation of America, 1815–1848* (New York: Oxford University Press, 2007), 314.

11. A concise treatment of different scholarly judgments of the book can be found in Grant Hardy, *Understanding the Book of Mormon: A Reader's Guide* (New York: Oxford University Press, 2010), xi–xiv.

12. "Taking the Scriptures to the World," *Ensign*, July 2001, 24.

13. "150 and Counting. The Book of Mormon Reaches Another Milestone," *The Church of Jesus Christ Newsroom* (April 18, 2011), Newsroom.lds.org/article/book-mormon-150-million.

14. Rodney Stark, *The Rise of Mormonism* (New York: Columbia University Press, 2005), 140–141.

15. David J. Whittaker, " 'That Most Important of All Books': A Printing History of the Book of Mormon," in *Occasional Papers* #5 (Provo, UT: The Neal A. Maxwell Institute for Religious Scholarship, 2007), 9. See also Larry E. Morris, comp., "Book of Mormon Chronology," in *Occasional Papers* #5 (Provo, UT: The Neal A. Maxwell Institute for Religious Scholarship, 2007), 5–7.

16. Richard Lyman Bushman, *Joseph Smith: Rough Stone Rolling. A Cultural Biography of Mormonism's Founder* (New York: Vintage, 2007), 83.

CHAPTER I
Joseph's Gold Bible

1. *Book of Mormon* (1830), title page. For a discussion of the phrase "author and proprietor" and its possible relationship to copyright issues of the time, see John W. Welch and Tim Rathbone, "Joseph Smith: 'Author and Proprietor,' " in *Reexploring the Book of Mormon*, ed. John W. Welch (Provo,

UT: Foundation for Ancient Research and Mormon Studies, 1992), 154–157.

2. Alan Taylor, "The Free Seekers: Religious Culture in Upstate New York, 1790–1835," *Journal of Mormon History* 27:1 (Spring 2000): 46.

3. Richard Lyman Bushman, *Joseph Smith: Rough Stone Rolling. A Cultural Biography of Mormonism's Founder* (New York: Vintage, 2007), 37; *Joseph Smith: History, Extracts from the History of Joseph Smith, the Prophet* (Salt Lake City, UT: Church of Jesus Christ of Latter-day Saints, 1982), 1:7.

4. Taylor, "The Free Seekers," 45.

5. Bushman, *Joseph Smith*, 36.

6. Taylor, "The Free Seekers," 52–53.

7. Bushman, *Joseph Smith*, 37.

8. *Joseph Smith: History*, 1:11.

9. A good treatment of the growing importance of the First Vision can be found in James B. Allen, "Emergence of a Fundamental: The Expanding Role of Joseph Smith's First Vision in Mormon Religious Thought," *Journal of Mormon History* 7 (1980): 43–61.

10. *Joseph Smith: History*, 1:30; Dean Jessee, "The Original Book of Mormon Manuscript," *BYU Studies* 10:3 (1969): 260.

11. *Joseph Smith: History*, 1:34.

12. Francis W. Kirkham, *Source Material concerning the Origin of the "Book of Mormon": America's Strangest Book* (n.p.: Francis Kirkham, 1937), 79.

13. Grant Hardy, ed., *The Book of Mormon: A Reader's Edition* (Urbana: University of Illinois Press, 2003), 643.

14. *Joseph Smith: History*, 1:35.

15. The best single essay on Joseph's early efforts to protect the plates is Andrew W. Hedges, " 'All My Endeavors to Preserve Them': Protecting the Plates in Palmyra, 22 Sep-

tember: December 1827," *Journal of Book of Mormon Studies* 8:2 (2001): 14–23.

16. Eber D. Howe, *Mormonism Unvailed: Or, A Faithful Account of that Singular Imposition and Delusion* (Painesville, OH: Eber D. Howe, 1834), 245–246. See also Bushman, *Joseph Smith*, 60.

17. William Mulder and A. Russell Mortenson, eds., *Among the Mormons: Historic Accounts by Contemporary Observers* (Lincoln: University of Nebraska Press, 1958), 30.

18. Bushman, *Joseph Smith*, 62.

19. Joel Tiffany, "Mormonism," *Tiffany's Monthly* 5 (August 1859): 170.

20. Isaac Hale, Affidavit, in Howe, *Mormonism Unvailed*, 264.

21. Lucy Mack Smith, *Biographical Sketches of Joseph Smith the Prophet and His Progenitors for Many Generations* (Liverpool: S. W. Richards, 1853), 113–114; Dan Vogel, *Joseph Smith: The Making of a Prophet* (Salt Lake City, UT: Signature Books, 2004), 113.

22. Brigham H. Roberts, *A Comprehensive History of The Church of Jesus Christ of Latter-Day Saints*, 6 vols. (Salt Lake City, UT: Deseret News Press, 1930), 1:101–109.

23. Vogel, *Joseph Smith*, 116.

24. Smith, *Biographical Sketches of Joseph Smith*, 115–117.

25. Ibid., 121–123. See also *Book of Mormon* (1830), 3–4.

26. *Doctrine and Covenants* 3 (July 1828).

27. Bushman, *Joseph Smith*, 70.

28. Jessee, "The Original Book of Mormon Manuscript," 259.

29. Bushman, *Joseph Smith*, 131; Joseph Knight Sr. "Joseph Knight's Recollection of Early Mormon History," ed. Dean C. Jessee, *BYU Studies* 17:1 (1976): 35.

30. James E. Lancaster, " 'By the Gift and Power of God': The Method of Translation of the Book of Mormon," *Saints Herald* 109 (November 15, 1962): 14–18, 22, 23.

31. Ethan Smith, *View of the Hebrews*, 2nd ed. (Poultney, VT: Smith & Shute, 1825); David Persuitte, *Joseph Smith and the Origins of "The Book of Mormon"*, 2nd ed. (Jefferson, NC: McFarland & Co., 2000), 125.

32. Terryl L. Givens, *The Book of Mormon: A Very Short Introduction* (New York: Oxford University Press, 2009), 98.

33. *Doctrine and Covenants* 8 and 9 (April 1829).

34. George Reynolds, *The Myth of the "Manuscript Found," or the Absurdities of the "Spaulding Story"* (n.p.: Juvenile Instructor Office, 1883), 79–80. See also Oliver Cowdery, "Council Bluffs (IA) Testimony, 21 October 1848," in *Early Mormon Documents*, ed. Dan Vogel, 5 vols. (Salt Lake City, UT: Signature Books, 1998), 2:494.

35. Howe, *Mormonism Unvailed*, 99.

36. *Book of Mormon* (1830), 589.

37. Vogel, *Joseph Smith*, 419–420.

38. Smith, *Biographical Sketches of Joseph Smith*, 148.

39. Russell R. Rich, "The Dogberry Papers and the Book of Mormon," *BYU Studies* 10:3 (1970): 319.

40. Royal Skousen, ed., *The Book of Mormon: The Earliest Text* (New Haven, CT: Yale University Press, 2009), xvi.

41. Ibid., xxix, xxx. See also Mulder and Mortenson, *Among the Mormons*, 42.

42. Knight, "Joseph Knight's Recollection of Early Mormon History," 36–37; Bushman, *Joseph Smith*, 81.

43. Smith, *Biographical Sketches of Joseph Smith*, 152.

44. Joseph Smith to N. C. Saxton, January 4, 1833, in Joseph Smith, Jr., *Personal Writings of Joseph Smith*, ed. Dean C. Jessee, rev. ed. (Salt Lake City, UT: Deseret Book, 2002), 297; Lucy Mack Smith, *The Revised and Enhanced History of Joseph*

Smith by His Mother, ed. Scot Facer Proctor and Maurine Jensen Proctor (Salt Lake City, UT: Bookcraft, 1996), 225.

45. Mark Twain, *Roughing It* (New York: Harper and Brothers, 1913), 110.

46. *Book of Mormon* (1830), 9.

47. The most sophisticated and comprehensive analysis of the *Book of Mormon* is Grant Hardy's *Understanding the Book of Mormon: A Reader's Guide* (New York: Oxford University Press, 2010).

48. *Book of Mormon* (1830), 116.

49. Mulder and Mortenson, *Among the Mormons*, 74.

CHAPTER 2
Holy Writ or Humbug?

1. "John H. Gilbert Interview, 1893," in *Early Mormon Documents*, ed. Dan Vogel, 5 vols. (Salt Lake City, UT: Signature Books, 1998), 2:551. For Gilbert's religious beliefs, see "Introduction to John H. Gilbert Collection," in Vogel, *Early Mormon Documents*, 2:515–516.

2. "John H. Gilbert Interview, 1893," in Vogel, *Early Mormon Documents*, 2:551.

3. Ibid.

4. Ibid.

5. Whitney R. Cross, *The Burned-Over District: The Social and Intellectual History of Enthusiastic Religion in Western New York, 1800–1850* (New York: Harper Torchbooks, 1965), 4.

6. Treatments of the religious fervor and diversity that characterized antebellum New England can be found in Nathan O. Hatch, *The Democratization of American Christianity* (New Haven, CT: Yale University Press, 1989); Ann Taves, *Fits, Trances, and Visions: Experiencing Religion and Explaining Experience from Wesley to James* (Princeton, NJ: Princeton University Press, 1999); Jon Butler, *Awash in a Sea*

of Faith: Christianizing the American People (Cambridge, MA: Harvard University Press, 1992); Stephen J. Stein, *The Shaker Experience in America* (New Haven, CT: Yale University Press, 1992); Paul E. Johnson and Sean Wilentz, *The Kingdom of Matthias: A Story of Sex and Salvation in 19th-Century America* (New York: Oxford University Press, 1994); and Ann Braude, *Radical Spirits: Spiritualism and Women's Rights in Nineteenth-Century America* (Boston, MA: Beacon Press, 1989).

7. *Messenger and Advocate*, October 1834, 14–15.

8. *Joseph Smith: History, Extracts from the History of Joseph Smith, the Prophet* (Salt Lake City, UT: Church of Jesus Christ of Latter-day Saints, 1982), 1:69.

9. Brigham H. Roberts, *A Comprehensive History of the Church of Jesus Christ of Latter-Day Saints*, 6 vols. (Salt Lake City, UT: Deseret News Press, 1930), 1:392.

10. Larry C. Porter, "Organizational Origins of the Church of Jesus Christ, 6 April 1830," in *Regional Studies in Latter-day Saint Church History: New York*, ed. Larry C. Porter et al. (Provo, UT: Department of Church History and Doctrine, Brigham Young University, 1992), 149–164. The competing view that the Church was actually founded at a meeting in Manchester, New York, is aptly presented in Michael H. Marquardt and Wesley P. Walters, *Inventing Mormonism: Tradition and the Historical Record* (San Francisco, CA: Smith Research Associates, 1994), 154–172.

11. Hatch, *The Democratization of American Christianity*, 113–122.

12. *Book of Mormon* (1830), 221–222.

13. *Book of Mormon* (1830), 164.

14. Steven C. Harper, "Missionaries in the American Religious Marketplace: Mormon Proselyting in the 1830s," *Journal of Mormon History* 24:2 (Fall 1998): 14,15.

15. Richard S. Van Wagoner, *Sidney Rigdon: A Portrait of Religious Excess* (Salt Lake City, UT: Signature Books, 1994), 26.

16. Daniel G. Reid, *Dictionary of American Christianity* (Downers Grove, IL: InterVarsity Press, 1990), 214.

17. Alexander Campbell, "Delusions," *Millennial Harbinger*, February 7, 1831, 91, 86.

18. Ibid., 91, 92.

19. Ibid., 93. *Book of Mormon* (1830), 240.

20. Campbell, "Delusions," 93.

21. The best overview of topics surrounding the historicity and authenticity of the *Book of Mormon* is a set of articles by the religious studies scholar John-Charles Duffy: John-Charles Duffy, "Mapping Book of Mormon Historicity Debates—Part I: A Guide for the Overwhelmed," *Sunstone* 151 (October 2008): 36–62; and "Mapping Book of Mormon Historicity Debates—Part II: Perspectives from the Sociology of Knowledge," *Sunstone* 152 (December 2008): 46–61.

22. Information about Joseph's translating the book can be found in an interview Joseph Smith III conducted with his mother, Emma, on February 4–10, 1879. The interview took place some fifty years after the events themselves, and it was published in the *Saints Herald*, October 1, 1879, 289–290.

23. Martin Harris is a good example of such steadfast testimony. Vogel, *Early Mormon Documents*, 2:296–297, 2:347.

24. Eber D. Howe, *Mormonism Unvailed* (Painesville, OH: Eber D. Howe, 1834), 232–269.

25. A Spalding manuscript titled "Manuscript Story" was discovered in Hawaii in 1884. Many believe this to be the "Manuscript Found" or a close variation of it. Over the years, several publishers have produced copies of the "Manuscript Story," many with the intent to show the differences between it and the *Book of Mormon*.

26. Howe, *Mormonism Unvailed*, 289–290.

27. The newspaper article is cited in Leonard J. Arrington, "James Gordon Bennett's 1831 Report on 'The Mormonites,'" *BYU Studies* 10 (Spring 1970): 5.

28. Ibid.

29. The level of Joseph's limited education and literacy is addressed in Dean C. Jessee, ed., *The Papers of Joseph Smith* (Salt Lake City, UT: Deseret Book Company, 1989), 1:xxi.

30. Richard Lyman Bushman, *Joseph Smith: Rough Stone Rolling. A Cultural Biography of Mormonism's Founder* (New York: Vintage, 2007), 19.

31. Van Wagoner, *Sidney Rigdon*, 133–134.

32. Wayne L. Cowdery et al., *Who Really Wrote the Book of Mormon?* (Santa Ana, CA: Vision House Publishers, 1977).

33. Matthew L. Jockers et al. "Reassessing Authorship of the *Book of Mormon* Using Delta and Nearest Shrunken Centroid Classification," *Literary and Linguistic Computing* 23:4 (2008): 482, 483.

34. I. Woodbridge Riley, *The Founder of Mormonism: A Psychological Study of Joseph Smith, Jr.* (New York: Dodd, Mead, and Co., 1902).

35. Lucy M. Smith, *The Revised and Enhanced History of Joseph Smith by His Mother*, ed. Scot Facer Proctor and Maurine Jensen Proctor (Salt Lake City, UT: Bookcraft, 1996), 112.

36. Fawn M. Brodie, *No Man Knows My History: The Life of Joseph Smith*, 2nd ed. (New York: Alfred A. Knopf, 1982), 442.

37. Ibid., ix, 69, 72–73, 80.

38. Ibid., 83.

39. Rick Grunder, *Mormon Parallels: A Bibliographic Source* (CD-rom), 1st ed.(LaFayette, NY: Rick Grunder, 2008).

40. David Persuitte, *Joseph Smith and the Origins of "The Book of Mormon"*, 2nd ed. (Jefferson, NC: McFarland & Co., 2000), 78.

41. Ibid., 83.

42. Ibid., 90.

43. William D. Morain, *The Sword of Laban: Joseph Smith, Jr. and the Dissociated Mind* (Washington D.C.: American Psychiatric Press, 1998), xx.

44. Ibid., xxiv.

45. Ibid., xxii–xxiii, 33.

46. Robert D. Anderson, *Inside the Mind of Joseph Smith: Psychobiography and the Book of Mormon* (Salt Lake City, UT: Signature Books, 1999), xii.

47. Ibid., xiii–xiv.

48. Ibid., xxxvii–xxxviii.

49. Ibid., 110–112.

50. Dan Vogel, *Joseph Smith: The Making of a Prophet* (Salt Lake City, UT: Signature Books, 2004), xiv–xv.

51. Ibid., xx.

52. Ibid., 166.

53. The story of Limhi is found in *Book of Mormon* (1830), 198–202.

54. Vogel, *Joseph Smith*, 167.

55. Ibid.

56. Ibid., xix.

CHAPTER 3
Multiplying Prophets

1. *Woman's Exponent* 7:7 (September 1, 1878): 51.

2. Joseph Smith, Jr., comp., *A Book of Commandments, For the Government of the Church of Christ, Organized According to the Law, on the 6th of April, 1830* (Zion, MO.: W. W. Phelps, 1833).

3. Joseph Smith, Jr. et al. *Doctrine and Covenants of the Church of the Latter-day Saints: From the Revelations of God* (Kirtland, OH: F. G. Williams and Co., 1835). One further indication that revelation was a dynamic process for

Joseph and his young Church is seen in how the *Doctrine and Covenants* was once again revised in 1844. Joseph Smith Jr., comp., *The Doctrine and Covenants of the Church of Jesus Christ of Latter-day Saints; Carefully Selected from the Revelations of God*, 2nd ed. (Nauvoo, IL: John Taylor, 1844).

4. The best treatments of Joseph's work on biblical revision are Robert J. Matthews, *"A Plainer Translation": Joseph Smith's Translation of the Bible* (Provo, UT: Brigham Young University Press, 1985); and Philip L. Barlow, *Mormons and the Bible: The Place of the Latter-day Saints in American Religion* (New York: Oxford University Press, 1991).

5. Joseph Smith, Jr., *History of the Church of Jesus Christ of Latter-day Saints*, ed. Brigham H. Roberts, 7 vols. (Salt Lake City, UT: Deseret Book Company, 1978), 4:461.

6. David J. Whittaker, "'That Most Important of All Books': A Printing History of the Book of Mormon," in *Occasional Papers* #5 (Provo, UT: The Neal A. Maxwell Institute for Religious Scholarship, 2007), 18; Richard P. Howard, *Restoration Scriptures: A Study of Their Textual Development*, 2nd ed. (Independence, MO: Herald Publishing House, 1995), 4–36.

7. Howard, *Restoration Scriptures*, 27.

8. Ibid., 33.

9. *Book of Mormon* (1830), 32; *Book of Mormon* (1837), 35.

10. The most complete discussion of the production of the 1840 edition can be found in Kyle R. Walker, "'As Fire Shut Up in My Bones': Ebenezer Robinson, Don Carlos Smith, and the 1840 Edition of the Book of Mormon," *Journal of Mormon History* 36 (Winter 2010): 1–40.

11. The most complete work done on *Book of Mormon* textual variants is the monumental study on the subject by Royal Skousen: *Analysis of Textual Variants of the Book of*

Mormon, Six Parts (Provo, UT: Foundation for Ancient Research and Mormon Studies, 2004–2009).

12. Walker, " 'As Fire Shut Up in My Bones,' " 18.

13. Robert Bruce Flanders, *Nauvoo: Kingdom on the Mississippi* (Urbana: University of Illinois Press, 1975), 41.

14. Leonard J. Arrington, *Brigham Young, American Moses* (New York: Alfred A. Knopf, 1985), 120.

15. Ernest H. Taves, *Trouble Enough: Joseph Smith and the Book of Mormon* (Buffalo, NY: Prometheus Books, 1984), 159–160.

16. Ibid., 160.

17. This argument is made most convincingly by Jan Shipps in her *Mormonism: The Story of a New Religious Tradition* (Urbana: University of Illinois Press, 1985), 41–85.

18. Brent Lee Metcalfe, ed., *New Approaches to the Book of Mormon* (Salt Lake City, UT: Signature Books, 1993), 96–103; Richard S. Van Wagoner, *Mormon Polygamy: A History*, 2nd ed. (Salt Lake City, UT: Signature Books, 1989), 3; Nathan O. Hatch, *The Democratization of American Christianity* (New Haven, CT: Yale University Press, 1989), 116.

19. Van Wagoner, *Mormon Polygamy*, 6.

20. Ibid., 21.

21. *Doctrine and Covenants* 132 (July 12, 1843); Van Wagoner, *Mormon Polygamy*, 3–4.

22. Richard Lyman Bushman, *Joseph Smith: Rough Stone Rolling. A Cultural Biography of Mormonism's Founder* (New York: Vintage, 2007), 437.

23. Arrington, *Brigham Young, American Moses*, 121.

24. Joseph Smith, Jr., *History of the Church of Jesus Christ of Latter-day Saints*, ed. Brigham H. Roberts, 7 vols. (Salt Lake City, UT: Deseret Book Company, 1978), 4:231; Joseph Fielding Smith, comp., *Teachings of the Prophet Joseph Smith* (Salt Lake City, UT: Deseret Book Company, 1976), 342–362.

25. Smith, *Teachings of the Prophet Joseph Smith*, 346; Bushman, *Joseph Smith*, 534–535.

26. Bushman, *Joseph Smith*, 538.

27. For some names of additional sects arising from Joseph Smith Jr.'s death, see Wayne A. Ham, "Center-Place Saints," in *Restoration Studies III: A Collection of Essays about the History, Beliefs, and Practices of the Reorganized Church of Jesus Christ of Latter Day Saints*, ed. Maurice L. Draper (Independence, MO: Herald Publishing House, 1986), 123; Paul K. Conkin, *American Originals: Homemade Varieties of Christianity* (Chapel Hill: University of North Carolina Press, 1997), 209. For the best overviews of different Mormon sects, see Newell G. Bringhurst and John C. Hamer, eds., *Scattering of the Saints: Schism within Mormonism* (Independence, MO: John Whitmer Books, 2007); Steven L. Shields, *Divergent Paths of the Restoration*, 4th ed. (Los Angeles, CA: Restoration Research, 1990).

28. Brigham H. Roberts, "Priesthood, and the Right of Succession," *Deseret News*, March 15, 1892, 2; Arrington, *Brigham Young, American Moses*, 114.

29. Arrington, *Brigham Young, American Moses*, 114–115; Roberts, "Priesthood, and the Right of Succession," 2.

30. Roberts ed., *History of the Church*, 7:233, 235.

31. Arrington, *Brigham Young, American Moses*, 116.

32. *The History of the Reorganized Church of Jesus Christ of Latter Day Saints*, 4 vols. (Independence, MO: Herald House, 1896), 3:74–77. A largely anecdotal history of the Bickertonite movement can be found in W. H. Cadman, *A History of the Church of Jesus Christ* (n.p.: Published by the Church, 1945).

33. *The Church of Jesus Christ General Business and Organization Conference Minutes* (Bridgewater, MI: The Church of Jesus Christ, 2007), 4399.

34. Roger Van Noord, *King of Beaver Island: The Life and Assassination of James Jesse Strang* (Urbana: University of Illinois Press, 1988), 53–56.

35. Ibid., 34–35.

36. *The History of the Reorganized Church*, 3:27.

37. Ibid., 3:29.

38. Conkin, *American Originals*, 205.

39. *The History of the Reorganized Church*, 3:33–35; Paul M. Edwards, *Our Legacy of Faith: A Brief History of the Reorganized Church of Jesus Christ of Latter Day Saints* (Independence, MO: Herald Publishing House, 1991), 122.

40. Edwards, *Our Legacy of Faith*, 136.

41. *The History of the Reorganized Church*, 3:205.

42. Edwards, *Our Legacy of Faith*, 125, 128.

43. Ibid., 129.

44. Ibid., 136, 144.

45. Ibid., 144, 161.

46. Ibid., 145.

47. Ibid., 162.

48. Howard, *Restoration Scriptures*, 38.

49. Edna K. Bush, "'And It Came to Pass': *The Book of Mormon*, RLDS 1966 Edition," *Dialogue: A Journal of Mormon Thought* 10:4 (Autumn 1977): 139.

50. Peggy Fletcher Stack, "RLDS Head Downplays His Role as Prophet," *Salt Lake Tribune*, June 29, 1996, D1.

51. William D. Russell, "The Last Smith Presidents and the Transformation of the RLDS Church," *Journal of Mormon History* 35:3 (Summer 2008): 46.

52. Ibid., 57.

53. Ibid., 66, 71, 73; Larry W. Conrad and Paul Shupe, "An RLDS Reformation? Construing the Task of RLDS Theology," *Dialogue: A Journal of Mormon Thought* 18:2 (Summer 1985): 93.

54. Russell, "The Last Smith Presidents," 77–80.

CHAPTER 4
Great Basin Saints and the Book

1. Joseph Smith, Jr., *History of the Church of Jesus Christ of Latter-day Saints*, ed. Brigham H. Roberts, 7 vols. (Salt Lake City, UT: Deseret Book Company, 1978), 6:548.

2. Leonard J. Arrington, *Great Basin Kingdom: Economic History of the Latter-Day Saints, 1830–1900* (Lincoln: University of Nebraska Press, 1958), 40–41.

3. *2009 Church Almanac: The Church of Jesus Christ of Latter-day Saints* (Salt Lake City, UT: Deseret News, 2009), 195.

4. Hugh Grant Stocks, "The Book of Mormon, 1830–1879: A Publishing History" (master's thesis, UCLA, 1979), 7.

5. Ibid., 13.

6. Ibid., 16–17.

7. Ibid., 17.

8. The one exception to this standardization was an 1869 edition of the book known as the Deseret alphabet edition. This edition was presented in a special phonetic alphabet developed for the Utah territory by Orson Pratt. Stocks, "The Book of Mormon, 1830–1879," 17–19.

9. See appendix 1 for a list of notable English-language versions of the *Book of Mormon*.

10. *Book of Mormon* (1830), 116.

11. Jerald and Sandra Tanner, *The Changing World of Mormonism* (Chicago, IL: Moody Press, 1980), 129, 183.

12. Stocks, "The Book of Mormon, 1830–1879," 104.

13. Peter Crawley, "Parley P. Pratt: Father of Mormon Pamphleteering," *Dialogue: A Journal of Mormon Thought* 15 (Autumn 1982): 13–26; David J. Whittaker, "Orson Pratt: Prolific Pamphleteer," *Dialogue: A Journal of Mormon Thought* 15 (Autumn 1982): 27–41; Orson Pratt, *Works of Orson Pratt* (Liverpool: R. James Printers, 1850), 33–48.

14. Breck England, *The Life and Thought of Orson Pratt* (Salt Lake City: University of Utah Press, 1985), 162.

15. Orson Pratt, *Divine Authenticity of the Book of Mormon* (Liverpool: R. James, 1850–1852), 35–36, 48.

16. Orson Pratt, *Masterful Discourses and Writings of Orson Pratt* (Salt Lake City, UT: Bookcraft, 1962), 419.

17. *Book of Mormon* (1849), title page.

18. Stocks, "The Book of Mormon, 1830–1879," 18–19, 109–110.

19. *Book of Mormon* (1879), 47, 53.

20. *Book of Mormon* (1920), 34, 393.

21. The specificity of Talmage's time line would come back to haunt Mormons in later decades as they found themselves forced to reconcile such conundrums as Joseph's declaration that the Mayan city of Palenque had been a Nephite city, even though the most reliable archaeological studies agree that Palenque was founded nearly two centuries after the Nephites had supposedly been destroyed by the Lamanites. Michael Coe, "Mormons and Archaeology: An Outside View," *Dialogue: A Journal of Mormon Thought* 8:2 (1973): 45.

22. Smith, *History of the Church*, 4:541.

23. Grant Underwood, "Book of Mormon Usage in Early LDS Theology," *Dialogue: A Journal of Mormon Thought* 17:3 (Autumn 1984): 52. For the place of the *Book of Mormon* in LDS teaching, see also Alton D. Merrill, "An Analysis of the Papers and Speeches of Those Who Have Written or Spoken about the Book of Mormon, Published during the Years 1830 to 1855 and 1915 to 1940, to Ascertain the Shift of Emphasis" (master's thesis, Brigham Young University, 1940).

24. Underwood, "Book of Mormon Usage," 53.

25. Ibid., 59.

26. Some discussion of doctrinal aspects of the *Book of Mormon* can be found in Terryl L. Givens, *By the Hand of Mormon: The American Scripture That Launched a New World Religion* (New York: Oxford University Press, 2002), 185–208.

27. Noel B. Reynolds, "The Coming Forth of the Book of Mormon in the Twentieth Century," *BYU Studies* 38:2 (1999): 23.

28. Ibid., 21.

29. Ibid., 11.

30. Allison D. Clark, "FARMS Preliminary Report on Missionary Plans and Materials Used by the Church of Jesus Christ of Latter-day Saints: 1900–1995" (unpublished manuscript deposited in the Special Collections of the Harold B. Lee Library, Brigham Young University), 1–2.

31. *Book of Mormon* (1981), Alma 22:32; Louis E. Hills, *Geography of Mexico and Central America from 2234 B.C. to 421 A.D.* (Independence, MO: n.p., 1917), 31.

32. Ferguson to David O. McKay, July 23, 1951, Ferguson Collection, Brigham Young University Library.

33. Stan Larson, "Thomas Stuart Ferguson and Book of Mormon Archaeology," in *Mormon Mavericks: Essays on Dissenters*, ed. John Sillito and Susan Staker (Salt Lake City, UT: Signature Books, 2002), 251.

34. Quoted in Stan Larson, "The Odyssey of Thomas Stuart Ferguson," *Dialogue: A Journal of Mormon Thought* (Spring 1990): 79.

35. Larson, "Thomas Stuart Ferguson and Book of Mormon Archaeology," 259.

36. Boyd Jay Petersen, *Hugh Nibley: A Consecrated Life* (Salt Lake City, UT: Greg Kofford Books, 2002), 231.

37. Hugh W. Nibley, *Lehi in the Desert*, in *The Collected Works of Hugh Nibley*, 19 vols. (Provo, UT: Deseret Book

and Foundation for Ancient Research and Mormon Studies, 1986–2010), 5:4.

38. Givens, *By the Hand of Mormon*, 119.

39. While Nibley absolutely towered within the Church as a Mormon scripture scholar without peer by the end of his career, he was not without his critics. Non-Mormon scholars, and even the occasional Mormon scholar, have been quick to point out that his method was so eclectic that it offered virtually meaningless evidence when it came to proving his arguments. One critic summed up the weakness of Nibley's research by arguing that Nibley tended to "gather sources from a variety of cultures all over the ancient world, lump them all together, and then pick and choose the bits and pieces" he wanted. In the eyes of his critics, Nibley had built his career on selecting stances and presuppositions that served his purposes, and ignored evidence and theories that did not. In the end, although even his detractors appreciated his brilliant intellect, they saw his work as driven by his religious agenda rather than a commitment to careful and objective scholarship. Kent P. Jackson, "HUGH NIBLEY. The Collected Works of Hugh Nibley," *BYU Studies* 28:4 (Fall 1988): 115.

40. Coe, "Mormons and Archaeology," 42; Richard N. Ostling and Joan K. Ostling, *Mormon America: The Power and the Promise* (San Francisco, CA: HarperCollins, 1999), 273.

41. S. Kent Brown, "'The Place That Was Called Nahom': New Light from Ancient Yemen," *Journal of Book of Mormon Studies* 8:1 (1999): 66–68; Givens, *By the Hand of Mormon*, 120.

42. Reynolds, "The Coming Forth of the Book of Mormon," 26.

43. Ibid., 13.

44. Ibid.

45. Ibid.,10.

46. Although Benson did not use this exact phrase at his first General Conference as the Church's highest leader, it would come to be a tagline intimately associated with his presidency. Two years after becoming Church president, Benson used the phrase in a speech later reprinted in the Church's magazine, the *Ensign*. Ezra Taft Benson, "Flooding the Earth with the Book of Mormon," *Ensign*, November 1988, 4.

47. Sheri L. Dew, *Ezra Taft Benson: A Biography* (Salt Lake City, UT: Deseret Book Company, 1987), 195.

48. Benson, "Flooding the Earth with the Book of Mormon," 4.

49. Ezra Taft Benson, "A Sacred Responsibility," *Ensign*, May 1986, 77.

50. Benson, "Flooding the Earth with the Book of Mormon," 4.

51. Reynolds, "The Coming Forth of the Book of Mormon," 31; Givens, *By the Hand of Mormon*, 242.

52. Gordon B. Hinckley, "A Testimony Vibrant and True," *Ensign*, August 2005, 6.

53. Larry E. Morris, comp., "Book of Mormon Chronology," in *Occasional Papers* #5 (Provo, UT: The Neal A. Maxwell Institute for Religious Scholarship, 2007), 4.

CHAPTER 5
Missionary Work and the Book

1. *Book of Mormon* (1830), 589.

2. Rodney Stark, *The Rise of Mormonism* (New York: Columbia University Press, 2005), 81; "Why Do They Do What They Do?" Newsroom, The Official Resources for the New Media, The Church of Jesus Christ of Latter-day Saints (June 25, 2007), http://www.lds.org/ldsnewsroom/eng/news-releases-stories/mormon-missionaries.

3. Stark, *The Rise of Mormonism*, 73–79.

4. Ibid., 81.

5. Quoted in Steven C. Harper, "Missionaries in the American Religious Marketplace: Mormon Proselyting in the 1830s," *Journal of Mormon History* 24:2 (Fall 1998) 28.

6. Brigham H. Roberts, *A Comprehensive History of the Church of Jesus Christ of Latter-Day Saints*, 6 vols. (Salt Lake City, UT: Deseret News Press, 1930), 1:225.

7. For a glimpse of the impressive conversion rates in England, see ibid., 3:403.

8. Leonard J. Arrington, *Great Basin Kingdom: Economic History of the Latter-Day Saints, 1830–1900* (Lincoln: University of Nebraska Press, 1958), 97.

9. Val G. Hemming, "A Voice from the Land of Zion: Elder Erastus Snow in Denmark, 1850–1852," *Dialogue: A Journal of Mormon Thought* 35 (March 2002): 135.

10. Roberts, *A Comprehensive History*, 3:391. For a list of foreign-language editions of the *Book of Mormon*, see appendix 2.

11. Roberts, *A Comprehensive History*, 3:394–395.

12. Larry E. Morris, "Book of Mormon Chronology," in *Occasional Papers* #5 (Provo, UT: The Neal A. Maxwell Institute for Religious Scholarship, 2007), 5.

13. *Book of Mormon* (1981), Alma 63:4–10; Spencer W. Kimball, "Of Royal Blood," *Ensign*, July 1971, 7.

14. Joseph Smith, Jr., *History of the Church of Jesus Christ of Latter-day Saints*, ed. Brigham H. Roberts, 7 vols., (Salt Lake City, UT: Deseret Book Company, 1978), 5:386, 404–405; S. George Ellsworth, ed., *The Journals of Addison Pratt* (Salt Lake City: University of Utah Press, 1990), xi.

15. Roberts, *A Comprehensive History*, 3:310.

16. Roberts, ed., *History of the Church*, 7:271–273.

17. Morris, "Book of Mormon Chronology," 5–6.

18. Email correspondence with Tod R. Harris, manager, Scripture Translation and Support, Translation Division, Church of Jesus Christ of Latter-day Saints (August 1, 2011). The set list for these partial translations was as follows: 1 Nephi 1–7 and 16–18; 2 Nephi 1–4, 5:1–20, 9, 29, 31–33; Enos (complete); Mosiah 2–5, 17, and 18; Alma 5, 11, 12, 32, 34, 39–42; Helman 13–16; 3 Nephi 1, 8, 11–30; 4 Nephi (complete); Mormon 1, 4, 6–9; Moroni (complete).

19. John E. Carr, "For in That Day…: A History of Translation and Distribution, 1965–1980" (unpublished typescript located in the LDS Church Translation Department), appendix 21 "President Kimball's Talk to the Regional Representatives."

20. Ibid. For Spencer Kimball's commitment to native populations of the Americas, see Edward L. Kimball, *Lengthen Your Stride: The Presidency of Spencer W. Kimball* (Salt Lake City, UT: Deseret Book, 2005), 288–295.

21. Morris, "Book of Mormon Chronology," 5–7. See appendix 2.

22. Armand L. Mauss, *All Abraham's Children: Changing Mormon Conceptions of Race and Lineage* (Urbana: University of Illinois Press, 2003), 213. For a discussion of the LDS Church's engagement with Africa as a mission field after the priesthood was opened to all "worthy males," see Kimball, *Lengthen Your Stride*, 236–245.

23. Mauss, *All Abraham's Children*, 212–217.

24. *The Book of Abraham*, 1:24; Smith, *History of the Church*, 2:438; Stephen R. Haynes, *Noah's Curse: The Biblical Justification of American Slavery* (New York: Oxford University Press, 2002), 23–40.

25. Wilford Woodruff, *Wilford Woodruff's Journal, 1833–1898: Typescript*, ed. Scott G. Kenney (Midvale, UT: Signature Books, 1983), 4:97.

26. *Book of Mormon* (1981), 2 Nephi 5:21.

27. *Book of Mormon* (1981), Alma 3:6.

28. Bruce McConkie, *Mormon Doctrine*, 2nd ed. (Salt Lake City, UT: Bookcraft, 1966), 527.

29. *Doctrine and Covenants* (1982), "Official Declaration—2," 294.

30. Carr, "For in That Day," appendix 22, "Formula for Emerging Language Priorities." Although this formula has changed over the years, the basic contours of the priorities set down in this appendix are still informative for the process today.

31. Daniel Radosh, "The Good Book Business," *New Yorker*, December 18, 2006, 56.

32. *Scripture Translation Manual*, "Scripture Translation Training" section (2009), 100. Copy of the manual found in the Translation Department of the Church of Jesus Christ of Latter-day Saints.

33. Ibid.

34. Email correspondence with Tod R. Harris, manager, Scripture Translation and Support, Translation Division, Church of Jesus Christ of Latter-day Saints (June 18, 2010).

35. *Preach My Gospel: A Guide to Missionary Service* (Salt Lake City: The Church of Jesus Christ of Latter-day Saints, 2004), 103.

36. Ibid., 109.

37. Ibid., 111.

38. *Book of Mormon* (1981), Moroni 10:4.

CHAPTER 6
Scholars and the Book

1. *Book of Mormon* (1981), Moroni 10:4.

2. *25 Years of Ancient Research and Mormon Studies* (n.p.: Foundation for Ancient Research and Mormon Studies, n.d.), 3.

3. John L. Sorenson, *An Ancient American Setting for the Book of Mormon* (Salt Lake City and Provo, UT: Deseret Book and Foundation for Ancient Research and Mormon Studies, 1996), 31–32. Other Sorenson works published by FARMS on the *Book of Mormon* include *Animals in the Book of Mormon: An Annotated Bibliography* (Provo, UT: Foundation for Ancient Research and Mormon Studies, 1992); "Fortifications in the Book of Mormon Account Compared with Mesoamerican Fortifications," in *Warfare in the Book of Mormon,* ed. Stephen D. Ricks and William J. Hamblin (Salt Lake City, UT: Deseret Book and Foundation for Ancient Research and Mormon Studies, 1990), 425–444; *Metals and Metallurgy Relating to the Book of Mormon Text* (Provo, UT: Foundation for Ancient Research and Mormon Studies, 1992); and *The Geography of Book of Mormon Events: A Source Book* (Provo, UT: Foundation for Ancient Research and Mormon Studies, 1992).

4. Sorenson, *An Ancient American Setting for the Book of Mormon,* 46–47.

5. Terryl L. Givens, *By the Hand of Mormon: The American Scripture That Launched a New World Religion* (New York: Oxford University Press, 2002), 101.

6. *Times and Seasons* 3:23 (October 1, 1842): 927. Such geographical identifications in Central America created certain problems for both Joseph and those who followed his line of thinking. Perhaps the most prominent of these was the fact that the Hill Cumorah, where Moroni had deposited the golden plates and where Joseph had recovered them centuries later, was located in upstate New York, not in Central America. To solve this seemingly insurmountable contradiction, Joseph began to develop what amounted to a double Cumorah thesis, which posited that there was indeed a Hill Cumorah near his boyhood home in Palmyra, but there was also a second Cumorah located near the Isthmus

of Tehuantepec in Central America. Givens, *By the Hand of Mormon*, 99.

7. Givens, *By the Hand of Mormon*, 128.

8. *Book of Mormon* (1981), introduction.

9. *25 Years of Ancient Research and Mormon Studies*, 6.

10. John C. Kunich, "Multiply Exceedingly: Book of Mormon Population Sizes," in *New Approaches to the Book of Mormon*, ed. Brent Lee Metcalfe (Salt Lake City, UT: Signature Books, 1993), 231–267; James E. Smith, "Nephi's Descendants? Historical Demography and the Book of Mormon," *FARMS Review of Books on the Book of Mormon* 6:1 (1994): 231–267; James E. Smith, "How Many Nephites? The Book of Mormon at the Bar of Demography," in *Book of Mormon Authorship Revisited*, ed. Noel B. Reynolds (Provo, UT : Foundation for Ancient Research and Mormon Studies, 1997), 255–294; William J. Hamblin, "Basic Methodological Problems with the Anti-Mormon Approach to the Geography and Archaeology of the Book of Mormon," *Journal of Book of Mormon Studies* 2:1 (1993): 161–197; John L. Sorenson and Robert F. Smith, "Barley in Ancient America," in *Reexploring the Book of Mormon*, ed. John Welch (Provo, UT: Foundation for Ancient Research and Mormon Studies, 1992): 130–132; John L. Sorenson and Robert F. Smith, "Once More: The Horse," in *Reexploring the Book of Mormon: The F.A.R.M.S. Updates*, ed. John Welch (Salt Lake City, UT: Deseret Book and Foundation for Ancient Research and Mormon Studies, 1992): 98–100; William Revell Phillips, "Metals in the Book of Mormon," *Journal of Book of Mormon Studies* 9:2 (2000): 36–43; Stephen D. Ricks and John A. Tvedtnes, "Jewish and Other Semitic Texts Written in Egyptian Characters," *Journal of Book of Mormon Studies* 5:2 (Fall 1996): 156–163; John A. Tvedtnes, "Hebrew Background of the Book of Mormon," in *Rediscovering the Book of Mormon*, ed. John L. Sorenson

and Melvin J. Thorne (Salt Lake City, UT: Deseret Book and Foundation for Ancient Research and Mormon Studies, 1991), 77–91; John Welch, *Chiasmus in Antiquity* (Provo, UT: Research Press, 1999).

11. Dan Egan, "BYU Gene Data May Shed Light on Origin of Book of Mormon's Lamanites," *Salt Lake Tribune*, November 30, 2000.

12. Thomas W. Murphy, "Lamanite Genesis Genealogy, and Genetics," in *American Apocrypha: Essays on the Book of Mormon*, ed. Dan Vogel and Brent Lee Metcalfe (Salt Lake City, UT: Signature Books, 2002), 47.

13. Robson Bonnichsen and D. Gentry Stelle, *Method and Theory for Investigating the Peopling of the Americas* (Corvallis, OR: Center for the Study of the First Americans, 1994); Michael Crawford, *The Origins of Native Americans: Evidence from Anthropological Genetics* (New York: Cambridge University Press, 1998); Simon G. Southerton, *Losing a Lost Tribe: Native Americans, DNA, and the Mormon Church* (Salt Lake City, UT: Signature Books, 2004).

14. Murphy, "Lamanite Genesis Genealogy, and Genetics," 48.

15. John Sorenson, "Problematic Role of DNA Testing in Unraveling Human History," *Journal of Book of Mormon Studies* 9:2 (2000): 66–74; Ryan Parr, "Missing the Boat to Ancient America…Just Plain Missing the Boat," *FARMS Review* 17:1 (2005): 83–106.

16. Royal Skousen, ed., *The Book of Mormon: The Earliest Text* (New Haven, CT: Yale University Press, 2009), xvi.

17. Ibid.

18. Ibid., xviii.

19. Ibid., xvii.

20. Royal Skousen, *Analysis of Textual Variants of the Book of Mormon*, Six Parts (Provo, UT: Foundation for Ancient Research and Mormon Studies, 2004–2009).

21. *Literature Books for Courses, 2011–2012: Penguin Group USA* (New York: Penguin, 2011), 4.

22. Givens, *By the Hand of Mormon*.

23. Grant Hardy, *Understanding the Book of Mormon: A Reader's Guide* (New York: Oxford University Press, 2010). Three other notable recent books from university presses include Clyde R. Forsberg, Jr., *Equal Rites: The Book of Mormon, Masonry, Gender, and American Culture* (New York: Columbia University Press, 2003); Richard Bushman, *Believing History: Latter-Day Saint Essays* (New York: Columbia University Press, 2007); and Terryl L. Givens, *The Book of Mormon: A Very Short Introduction* (New York: Oxford University Press, 2009).

24. Gordon S. Wood, "Evangelical America and Early Mormonism," *New York History* 61 (1980): 381.

CHAPTER 7
Illustrating the Book

1. Ezra Taft Benson, "Flooding the Earth with the Book of Mormon," *Ensign*, November 1988, 4.

2. George Reynolds, *A Complete Concordance of the Book of Mormon* (Salt Lake City, UT: Deseret Book Company, 1957); Bruce A. Van Orden, *Prisoner for Conscience' Sake: The Life of George Reynolds* (Salt Lake City, UT: Deseret Book, 1992), 114.

3. Van Orden, *Prisoner for Conscience' Sake*, 53, 186.

4. Ibid., 152.

5. Noel A. Carmack, " 'A Picturesque and Dramatic History': George Reynolds's *Story of the Book of Mormon*," *BYU Studies* 47:2 (2008): 134.

6. George Reynolds, *The Story of the Book of Mormon*, 5th ed. (Chicago, IL: Hillison & Etten, 1888), iii.

7. Van Orden, *Prisoner for Conscience' Sake*, 152.

8. "Zarahemla," *Times and Seasons* 3:23 (October 1, 1842): 927.

9. *Book of Mormon* (1879), 155.

10. Reynolds, *The Story of the Book of Mormon*, 14.

11. Ibid., iv.

12. "To the Artists of Utah," *Deseret Weekly*, March 8, 1890, 23.

13. Reynolds, *The Story of the Book of Mormon*, 201.

14. By the 1880s, Ottinger had already painted a number of pictures set in ancient America and had even become a respected lecturer on Mesoamerican culture because of the detailed research he had completed in order to lend his paintings the greatest possible realism. Heber G. Richards, "George M. Ottinger, Pioneer Artist of Utah," *Western Humanities Review* 3:3 (July 1949): 212–213, 216.

15. John L. Stephens, *Incidents of Travel in Central America, Chiapas and Yucatan* (New York: Harper & Brothers, 1841), 1:frontispiece. Carmack, "'A Picturesque and Dramatic History,'" 123–124.

16. Genet Bingham Dee, *A Voice from the Dust: A Sacred History of Ancient Americans* (Salt Lake City, UT: Deseret News Press, 1939), 2, 40, 240, 250, 272, 372, 375, 387, 447, 458, 562, 605, 619, 621, 645, 648, 651, 660, 671, 685, 766, 771, 773, 776, 782–783, 786, 788, 814. One representative example of Mesoamerican illustrative art in this series can be found in Clinton F. Larson, *Illustrated Stories from the Book of Mormon, Mosiah 1 through Mosiah 17*, vol. 6 (Provo, UT: Promised Land Publications, 1970), 31–32, 42, 45, 47, 63, 67.

17. Minerva Teichert to Rosa Gold, undated letter, Laurie Teichert Eastwood Collection on Minerva Kohlepp Teichert, Special Collections, Harold B. Lee Library, Brigham Young University, MS 2243, Box 2, Folder 11.

18. As quoted in John W. Welch and Doris R. Dant, *The Book of Mormon Paintings of Minerva Teichert* (Salt Lake City, UT: Bookcraft, 1997), 11, 162–168.

19. Jan Underwood Pinborough, "Minerva Kohlhepp Teichert: With a Bold Brush," *Ensign*, April 1989, 34.

20. Welch and Dant, *The Book of Mormon Paintings*, 32.

21. Ibid., 34.

22. As evidence of her familiarity with the *Book of Mormon*, notes that she made concerning the text can be found in a folder entitled "The Story of the Book of Mormon," Laurie Teichert Eastwood Collection on Minerva Kohlepp Teichert, Special Collections, Harold B. Lee Library, Brigham Young University, MS 2243, Box 5, Folder 9.

23. *Book of Mormon* (1981), Alma 53:16–21, 56:47–48.

24. *Book of Mormon* (1981), Alma 47:22–35.

25. Welch and Dant, *The Book of Mormon Paintings*. Also important to the popularizing of Teichert's art was the appearance of the *Book of Mormon: Heirloom Edition* (Salt Lake City, UT: Deseret Book Company, 2011) that reproduced fifty full-color Teichert paintings as illustrations for the sacred text.

26. *Book of Mormon* (1963), opening illustrations and their captions.

27. Good treatments of Friberg's training and career include Robert T. Barrett and Susan Easton Black, "Setting the Standard in LDS Art: Four Illustrators of the Mid-Twentieth Century," *BYU Studies* 44:2 (2005): 25–80; and Ted Schwarz, *Arnold Friberg: The Passion of a Modern Master* (Flagstaff, AZ: Northland Press, 1985).

28. As quoted in Barrett and Black, "Setting the Standard in LDS Art," 32.

29. Ibid., 75.

30. Two good overviews of Friberg's Howells commission can be found in Schwarz, *Arnold Friberg*, 49–55, and Vern G.

Swanson, "The Book of Mormon Art of Arnold Friberg: 'Painter of Scripture,'" *Journal of Book of Mormon Studies* 10:1 (2001): 26–35.

31. Ibid., 57–75.

32. Barrett and Black, "Setting the Standard in LDS Art," 35.

33. Swanson, "The Book of Mormon Art of Arnold Friberg," 34.

34. As quoted in Barrett and Black, "Setting the Standard in LDS Art," 33.

35. Deanna Draper Buck, *My First Book of Mormon Stories* (Salt Lake City, UT: Deseret Book Company, 2001); Kimberly Jensen Bowman, *Jr. Book of Mormon: A Pictorial Study-Guide for Children* (Springville, UT: Cedar Fort, 2001); David Bowman, *Who's Your Greatest Hero? Jesus Visits the Nephites* (Salt Lake City, UT: Shadow Mountain, 2009), 2, 6, 13, 26.

36. Michael D. Allred, *The Golden Plates*, vol. 1, *The Sword of Laban and the Tree of Life* (Lakeside, OR: AAA POP, 2004), cover.

37. Michael D. Allred, *The Golden Plates,* vol. 2, *The Liahona and the Promised Land* (Lakeside, OR: AAA POP, 2005), 95, 111, 120, 125; Michael D. Allred, *The Golden Plates*, vol. 3, *The Lord of the Vineyard and Discovering Zarahemla* (Lakeside, OR: AAA POP, 2005), 180.

38. Allred, *The Golden Plates*, vol. 3, inside front cover.

CHAPTER 8
The Book on Screen and Stage

1. William A. Morton to A.J.T. Sorensen, July 15, 1915, LDS Church Archives, MS 18203, Folder 2.

2. William A. Morton to A.J.T. Sorensen, August 18, 1915, LDS Church Archives, MS 18203, Folder 2.

3. William A. Morton to A.J.T. Sorensen, July 15, 1915, LDS Church Archives, MS 18203, Folder 2.

4. An outline for the film's script can be found in a series of film treatment notes located in the LDS Church Archives, MS 18203, Folder 3, pp. 18–27.

5. B. H. Roberts, *Corianton: A Nephite Story* (Salt Lake City, UT: n.p., 1902). Orestes Utah Bean (1873–1937) produced a successful theatrical version of Roberts's story entitled *Corianton: An Aztec Romance* that played both in Salt Lake City and even for a short time (eight performances during September 1912) at the Manhattan Opera House in New York City.

6. Corianton Corporation Letter from Lester Park, June 30, 1931, to Mr. Andrew Steedman, BYU Special Collections, Andrew Steedman Collection, MS 3731.

7. Ibid.

8. Ibid.

9. It is estimated that the film cost $200,000 to make, a fantastic sum for an independent film company such as Park's during America's Great Depression. The film did play limited engagements, after its run in Salt Lake City, in Provo and Ogden. It was bought by a distributor and rereleased sometime later in California under the title *Love's Temptation.*

10. Randy Astle, "A History of Mormon Cinema," *BYU Studies* 46:2 (2007): 104.

11. Jeff Vice, "Book of Mormon Coming to Silver Screen," *Deseret News*, November 1, 2002, http://deseret-news.com/dn/view/0,1249,415016596,00.html.

12. Doug Gibson, "Political Surf on How to Make a Book of Mormon Movie," *Standard-Examiner Blogs*, May 1, 2009, http://blogs.standard.net/2009/05/political-surf-on-how-to-make-a-book-of-mormon-movie/.

13. Film costs and revenues taken from www.boxofficemojo.com, http://www.brandongray.com/movies/?id=bookofmormonmovie.htm.

14. Letter from Charles W. Whitman to Ira J. Markham, January 20, 1965, Ira J. Markham Manuscript Collection, BYU Harold B. Lee Library, Special Collections, MS 43; "Summary of Events in Connection with the Beginning and the Development of the Hill Cumorah Pageant, 'America's Witness for Christ,'" Prepared January 23, 1960, by Ira J. and Beatrice Parson Markham, pp. 4, 6, Ira J. Markham Manuscript Collection, BYU Harold B. Lee Library, Special Collections, MS 43.

15. Gerald S. Argetsinger, "The Hill Cumorah Pageant: A Historical Perspective," *Journal of Book of Mormon Studies* 13:1–2 (2004): 59.

16. Richard N. Ostling and Joan K. Ostling, *Mormon America: The Power and the Promise* (San Francisco, CA: HarperCollins, 1999), 243; Argetsinger, "The Hill Cumorah Pageant," 99.

17. Press Kit, Hill Cumorah Pageant, 1962, Twenty-fifth Anniversary, BYU Harold B. Lee Library, Special Collections, American Folio, AC 901.A1, no. 439; Ostling and Ostling, *Mormon America*, 243.

18. A good discussion of these changes can be found in Charles Walker Whitman, "A History of the Hill Cumorah Pageant (1937–1964) and an Examination of the Dramatic Development of the Text of *America's Witness for Christ*" (PhD diss., University of Minnesota, 1967), 200–368. For modern changes to the script, see Argetsinger, "The Hill Cumorah Pageant," 64.

19. Argetsinger, "The Hill Cumorah Pageant," 64.

20. Trey Parker, Robert Lopez, and Matt Stone, *The Book of Mormon* (New York: Newmarket Press, 2011), v, vi.

21. Adam Markovitz, "'Book of Mormon' Soundtrack Reaches Number Three on Billboard Albums Chart, Bested Only by Gaga and Adele," June 12, 2011, http://music-mix.ew.com/2011/06/15/book-mormon-soundtrack-billboard/.

22. Parker, Lopez, and Stone, *The Book of Mormon*, 35.

23. Ibid.

24. Ibid., 91.

EPILOGUE

1. *Book of Mormon* (1981), 3 Nephi 26:6

APPENDIX I
Notable *Book of Mormon* Editions in English

1. Information collated and condensed from the work done in Larry E. Morris, comp., "Book of Mormon Chronology," in *Occasional Papers* #5 (Provo, UT: The Neal A. Maxwell Institute for Religious Scholarship, 2007), 2–7.

FURTHER READING

BIOGRAPHIES OF JOSEPH SMITH JR.

Brodie, Fawn M. *No Man Knows My History: The Life of Joseph Smith*. 2nd ed. New York: Alfred A. Knopf, 1982.

Bushman, Richard Lyman. *Joseph Smith: Rough Stone Rolling: A Cultural Biography of Mormonism's Founder*. New York: Vintage, 2007.

Hill, Donna. *Joseph Smith: The First Mormon*. Salt Lake City, UT: Signature Books, 1999.

Remini, Robert Vincent. *Joseph Smith*. New York: Viking, 2002.

Vogel, Dan. *Joseph Smith: The Making of a Prophet*. Salt Lake City, UT: Signature Books, 2004.

BIOGRAPHIES OF IMPORTANT MORMON FIGURES

Arrington, Leonard J. *Brigham Young, American Moses*. New York: Alfred A. Knopf, 1985.

Dew, Sheri L. *Ezra Taft Benson: A Biography*. Salt Lake City, UT: Deseret Book Company, 1987.

England, Breck. *The Life and Thought of Orson Pratt*. Salt Lake City: University of Utah Press, 1985.

Kimball, Edward L. *Lengthen Your Stride: The Presidency of Spencer W. Kimball.* Salt Lake City, UT: Deseret Book, 2005.

Launius, Roger D. *Joseph Smith III: Pragmatic Prophet.* Urbana: University of Illinois Press, 1995.

Newell, Linda King, and Valeen Tippetts Avery. *Mormon Enigma: Emma Hale Smith.* 2nd ed. Urbana: University of Illinois Press, 1994.

Petersen, Boyd Jay. *Hugh Nibley: A Consecrated Life.* Salt Lake City, UT: Greg Kofford Books, 2002.

Prince, Gregory A., and Wm. Robert Wright. *David O. McKay and the Rise of Modern Mormonism.* Salt Lake City: University of Utah Press, 2005.

Schwarz, Ted. *Arnold Friberg: The Passion of a Modern Master.* Flagstaff, AZ: Northland Press, 1985.

Van Noord, Roger. *King of Beaver Island: The Life and Assassination of James Jesse Strang.* Urbana: University of Illinois Press, 1988.

Van Orden, Bruce A. *Prisoner for Conscience' Sake: The Life of George Reynolds.* Salt Lake City, UT: Deseret Book, 1992.

Van Wagoner, Richard S. *Sidney Rigdon: A Portrait of Religious Excess.* Salt Lake City, UT: Signature Books, 1994.

WORKS ON THE *BOOK OF MORMON*

Bush, Edna K. "'And It Came to Pass': *The Book of Mormon*, RLDS 1966 Edition." *Dialogue: A Journal of Mormon Thought* 10:4 (Autumn 1977): 139–142.

Bushman, Richard. *Believing History: Latter-Day Saint Essays.* New York: Columbia University Press, 2007.

Carmack, Noel A. "'A Picturesque and Dramatic History': George Reynolds's *Story of the Book of Mormon*." *BYU Studies* 47:2 (2008): 115–141.

242   FURTHER READING

Duffy, John-Charles. "Mapping Book of Mormon Historicity Debates—Part I: A Guide for the Overwhelmed." *Sunstone* 151 (October 2008): 36–62.

———. "Mapping Book of Mormon Historicity Debates—Part II: Perspectives from the Sociology of Knowledge." *Sunstone* 152 (December 2008): 46–61.

Forsberg, Clyde R., Jr. *Equal Rites: The Book of Mormon, Masonry, Gender, and American Culture.* New York: Columbia University Press, 2003.

Givens, Terryl L.. *The Book of Mormon: A Very Short Introduction.* New York: Oxford University Press, 2009.

———. *By the Hand of Mormon: The American Scripture That Launched a New World Religion.* New York: Oxford University Press, 2002.

Gutjahr, Paul C. "The Golden Bible in the Bible's Golden Age: *The Book of Mormon* in Antebellum Print Culture." *American Transcendental Quarterly*, n.s., 12:4 (1998): 275–293.

Hardy, Grant, ed. *The Book of Mormon: A Reader's Edition.* Urbana: University of Illinois Press, 2003.

———. *Understanding the Book of Mormon: A Reader's Guide.* New York: Oxford University Press, 2010.

Jessee, Dean. "The Original Book of Mormon Manuscript." *BYU Studies* 10:3 (1969): 259–278.

Jockers, Matthew L., et al. "Reassessing Authorship of the *Book of Mormon* Using Delta and Nearest Shrunken Centroid Classification." *Literary and Linguistic Computing* 23:4 (2008): 465–491.

Metcalfe, Brent Lee, ed. *New Approaches to the Book of Mormon.* Salt Lake City, UT: Signature Books, 1993.

Ostler, Blake T. "The Book of Mormon as a Modern Expansion of an Ancient Source." *Dialogue: A Journal of Mormon Thought* 20:1 (1987): 66–91.

Rees, Robert A., and Eugene England. *The Reader's Book of Mormon*. 7 vols. Salt Lake City, UT: Signature Books, 2008.

Reynolds, Noel B. "The Coming Forth of the Book of Mormon in the Twentieth Century." *BYU Studies* 38:2 (1999): 7–47.

Sorenson, John L. *An Ancient American Setting for the Book of Mormon*. Salt Lake City and Provo, UT: Deseret Book and Foundation for Ancient Research and Mormon Studies, 1996.

Vogel, Dan, and Lee Metcalfe, eds. *American Apocrypha*. Salt Lake City, UT: Signature Books, 2002.

Walker, Kyle R. "'As Fire Shut Up in My Bones': Ebenezer Robinson, Don Carlos Smith, and the 1840 Edition of the Book of Mormon." *Journal of Mormon History* 36 (Winter 2010): 1–40.

Welch, John W., ed. *Reexploring the Book of Mormon*. Provo, UT: Foundation for Ancient Research and Mormon Studies, 1992.

Welch, John W., and Doris R. Dant. *The Book of Mormon Paintings of Minerva Teichert*. Salt Lake City, UT: Bookcraft, 1997.

Whittaker, David J. "That Most Important of All Books: A Printing History of the Book of Mormon." In *Occasional Papers* #5, 9–32. Provo, UT: The Neal A. Maxwell Institute for Religious Scholarship, 2007.

WORKS ON MORMONISM MORE GENERALLY

Astle, Randy, with Gideon O. Burton. "A History of Mormon Cinema." *BYU Studies* 46:2 (2007): 12–163.

Barlow, Philip. *Mormons and the Bible: The Place of the Latter-day Saints in American Religion*. New York: Oxford University Press, 1991.

Barrett, Robert T., and Susan Easton Black. "Setting the Standard in LDS Art: Four Illustrators of the Mid-Twentieth Century." *BYU Studies* 44:2 (2005): 25–80.

Bringhurst, Newell G., and John C. Hamer, eds. *Scattering of the Saints: Schism within Mormonism*. Independence, MO: John Whitmer Books, 2007.

Edwards, Paul M. *Our Legacy of Faith: A Brief History of the Reorganized Church of Jesus Christ of Latter Day Saints*. Independence, MO: Herald Publishing House, 1991.

The History of the Reorganized Church of Jesus Christ of Latter Day Saints. 4 vols. Independence, MO: Herald House, 1896.

Mauss, Armand L. *All Abraham's Children: Changing Mormon Conceptions of Race and Lineage*. Urbana: University of Illinois Press, 2003.

Ostling, Richard N. and Joan K. *Mormon America: The Power and the Promise*. San Francisco, CA: HarperCollins, 1999.

Roberts, Brigham H. *A Comprehensive History of The Church of Jesus Christ of Latter-Day Saints, Century I*. 6 vols. Salt Lake City, UT: Deseret News Press, 1930.

Shipps, Jan. *Mormonism: The Story of a New Religious Tradition*. Urbana: University of Illinois Press, 1985.

Stark, Rodney. *The Rise of Mormonism*. New York: Columbia University Press, 2005.

Van Wagoner, Richard S. *Mormon Polygamy: A History*. 2nd ed. Salt Lake City, UT: Signature Books, 1989.

IMPORTANT REFERENCE WORKS ON MORMONISM
AND THE *BOOK OF MORMON*

Grunder, Rick. *Mormon Parallels: A Bibliographic Source*. CD-rom. 1st ed. LaFayette, NY: Rick Grunder, 2008.

Howard, Richard P. *Restoration Scriptures: A Study of Their Textual Development*. 2nd ed. Independence, MO: Herald Publishing House, 1995.

Ludlow, Daniel H., ed. *Encyclopedia of Mormonism*. 4 vols. New York: Macmillan, 1992.

Parry, Donald W., Jeanette W. Miller, and Sandra A. Thorne, eds. *A Comprehensive Annotated Book of Mormon Bibliography*. Provo, UT: Research Press, 1996.

Stocks, Hugh Grant. "The Book of Mormon, 1830–1879: A Publishing History." Master's thesis, University of California, Los Angeles, 1979.

———. "The Book of Mormon in English, 1870–1920: A Publishing History and Analytical Bibliography." PhD diss., University of California, Los Angeles, 1986.

Whittaker, David J. *Mormon Americana: A Guide to Sources and Collections in the United States*. Provo, UT: BYU Studies, 1995.

Book of Lehi, 4, 20, 26

Book of Mormon: and action
figures, 199; and archaeology, 100–103, 165–166;
authorship of, 45–58;
binding of, 5, 132–133;
British editions of, 87–89,
93, 201–202; changes in
the text of, 63–64, 90–91,
95–98; chiasmic structure
of, 129; and Christol-
ogy, 8; copyright of, 31,
198–199, 210n1; Danish
translation of, 116–117;
Deseret translation of,
93–94, 223n8; distribu-
tion of, 9, 87–88, 132–136;
footnotes in, 95, 97;
foreign-language transla-
tion of, 116–120, 123–131,
205–208; formatting of,
88–98, 149; index in, 88;
Japanese edition of, 131,
198; limited geography
theory of, 141–143; mis-
sionary use of, 113–136;
modern-language version
of, 83, 202; narrative structure of, 34, 151; paper used
in, 132; printing of, 5, 9,
29–32, 87–92, 117, 131, 198;
purity of, 37; quad format
of, 203; RLDS editions
of, 82–83, 199, 202; RLDS
position on, 81–85; Span-
ish translation of, 125–126;
status of in American
society, 9, 150–152, 195;
stereotyped editions of,
89, 91; title page of, 6,
30; translation of into
English, 5, 16, 18–26, 83,
127; triple format of, 203;
usage of among Mormons,
84–85, 96–100, 105–109,
134–136; witnesses to,
28, 46

The Book of Mormon, the
Broadway musical,
192–195

*The Book of Mormon Movie,
Vol. 1: The Journey*, 185–188

Book of the Law of the Lord, 75

Booth, Ezra, 47

Bora Bora, 118

Borturini Codex, 156–157

Botswana, 123

Bowman, David, 175

Bowman, Kimberly Jensen,
175

Briggs, Jason, 77–79

Brigham Young University,
100–102, 104, 106, 108,
138, 143–144, 146

British Mission, 93, 116

Brodie, Fawn, 52

Buck, Deanna Draper, 175

Buddhism, 10

Buffalo, New York, 115

burned-over district, 39